A Preface: Why I Wrote This Book

When people imagine the life of a sportswriter, they undoubtedly gravitate to the more glamorous aspects – sitting courtside for an NCAA tournament buzzer-beater, or standing on the Rose Bowl sideline as Vince Young scampers right past you for the game-winning touchdown against USC. I've experienced both those moments and many others for which I'm eternally grateful. However, I've also spent at least a couple hundred hours of my life in hotel lobbies and hallways across America waiting for middle-aged men in suits – mainly conference commissioners and athletic directors – to emerge from a meeting room. Not that I expect pity. When these guys get together they generally do so at The Four Seasons in Dallas, the Langham in Pasadena, the Biltmore in Phoenix and other such luxury venues. There are worse places to kill time … before returning to my room at the Courtyard by Marriott down the street.

I'll never forget the April 2008 BCS meetings, held that year at the Westin Diplomat in Hollywood, Florida. Typically, the other media members and I resort to chasing down one of the commissioners as he's racing to catch a flight home and sticking a recorder in his face, but on this rare occasion, the newsmakers came to us. Four months earlier I'd written a lengthy story on SEC commissioner Mike Slive's attempt to persuade his colleagues to adopt what was then called a Plus-One (essentially, a four-team playoff). He had the support of ACC counterpart John Swofford, while others said they were open to a discussion. Now, as we sat in front of our laptops around a long rectangular conference table, the commissioners entered in groups of two or three to explain why they'd just resoundingly shot down Slive's proposal following what I'd soon learn was a very brief conversation. The proposal was dead on arrival.

"Our league is just not favorable to a playoff system at all and viewed this as a first step in that direction," said then-Big 12 commissioner Dan Beebe.

"The seeded model that's been discussed looked like a playoff to us, and we don't think a playoff is in the best interest of college football," said Big East commissioner Mike Tranghese. (Tranghese, now retired, is a member of the first-ever playoff selection committee. Of course.)

Slive, who first began his campaign after undefeated SEC champion Auburn's exclusion from the title game in 2004, spent much of the session standing against a wall in the back of the room looking dejected.

By then the clamor to scrap the BCS for a playoff had been in full force for many years, and I'd devoted many an SI.com Mailbag – not to mention an entire chapter of my 2007 book, *Bowls, Polls and Tattered Souls* – trying to explain why fans taking this position shouldn't hold their breath. But nothing I wrote could come close to conveying just how firmly entrenched the BCS was. You really had to

The Thinking Fan's Guide
to the
College Football Playoff

Stewart Mandel

ISBN: 1500102482
ISBN-13: 9781500102487

Table of Contents

be sitting in the room that day and watch this parade of commissioners so brusquely dismiss even entertaining a playoff proposal.

Yet four years later, again at the Westin Diplomat, the narrative had completely changed. Following three days of meetings, the commissioners had agreed to forward various four-team proposals to their conference athletic directors and presidents. They'd even stopped hiding behind the deceptive Plus-One moniker. "We have agreed to use the P-word," said Pac-12 Commissioner Larry Scott – by which he meant playoff.

There was no turning back now.

By then the commissioners had already held three previous meetings on the subject, beginning in New Orleans the morning after a polarizing BCS championship game rematch between Alabama and LSU. I'd been there to cover two of them, and I'd be there for many more, first as the group formally agreed to the format (Chicago, June 20, 2012) and then, over the next two years, as they hashed out the various details.

All told, between January 2012 and May 2014, I had the privilege of camping out in the lobbies of nine different properties. What can I say? Some college football media members can't get enough of recruiting, the coaching carousel, realignment or 40 times. I'm a BCS governance junkie. I have an unquenchable thirst for recusal policies, host bowls and revenue distributions. So over the course of two-plus years I gained a pretty good grasp of the ins and outs of the system that would eventually be called – wait for it – the College Football Playoff.

But I also realize that the vast majority of fans have not been following every minute step of the new entity's evolution, and who could blame them? They have jobs. And lives. Not to mention much of the discussion has been chronicled primarily in 140-character tidbits. Perhaps you remember seeing something at some point about the bowl selection process, but the next second someone tweeted a hilarious Photoshop of Jameis Winston holding crab legs above his head and whoops – what was that about the playoff?

The fact is, for such a seemingly simple concept – four teams playing a two-week tournament to determine the national champion – the College Football Playoff is in fact extremely confusing, arguably even more so than the BCS. This realization first hit me when my wife and I had dinner with good friends shortly before I left to cover the January 2014 bowls. This couple were not hardcore football fans by any means, but they were aware enough to know the postseason was changing the next year. After asking a series of questions about the Rose Bowl's place in the new system, the husband eventually said, "You know – you ought to write an e-book explaining all of this."

I thought, "Huh – other than the fact I have no idea how to publish an e-book, that's a good idea." I filed it away for a couple of months, but the more I interacted with readers via the Mailbag or Twitter, the more I realized how foreign the playoff remains to so much of the public. At one point I bounced the book concept by a friend in the media whom I consider to be highly knowledgeable about college football. "I just get the sense there are a lot of things people don't realize yet," I said. "Like the fact the selection committee is picking the teams for the other major bowls, too." There was a brief silence on the other end. "Until you just said that, I had no idea myself."

Was that news to you as well? No problem. I'm going to get to that. By the time you're finished reading this book, you, too, will be an expert in all aspects of the new College Football Playoff. I'll explain the rotation process by which six major bowls will take turns hosting a new semifinal doubleheader and the details of the new stand-alone national championship game. I'll discuss the trickle-down changes to the larger bowl system. I'll introduce the members and examine the process by which the first-ever FBS selection committee will conduct their momentous task. And I'll provide a glimpse into the differences in the new selection process by applying it to seasons past.

Feel free to send me retroactive hate mail for your favorite team's imaginary exclusion from the 2010 playoff field.

This being college football, you may find yourself scratching your head at various junctures. You may need to reread a certain passage a couple of times. Don't feel bad. Even the people that work in college football don't fully understand this thing yet. I hope my little book will ultimately prove helpful and educational – starting with a brief history lesson.

What Took So Long?

Princeton and Rutgers staged the first college football game on November 6, 1869. It only took 145 years for the sport's highest level to adopt a four-team playoff. In the interim, generations of newspaper columnists and sports talk hosts have made a healthy living asking some variation of the following question: "Why doesn't college football have a playoff like every other sport???"

Well, to begin with, bowl games – college football's unique season crescendo – predate any major American sport's playoff. The first Rose Bowl was played on January 1, 1902. The first World Series was played 21 months later, and technically it was not a playoff, but a best-of-nine series between two teams. The first NHL playoffs commenced in 1918, while the first NFL playoff game did not occur until 1932. The NCAA staged its first basketball tournament in 1939, the NBA its first playoff series in 1947. Even Super Bowl I on January 15, 1967, was not actually called the Super Bowl at the time. Its official title was the NFL-AFL World Championship Game. The fact that the NFL later adopted college football's vernacular rather than vice versa shows just how exalted bowl games were for much of the 20th century.

Furthermore, college football began primarily as a regional sport – Eastern teams (e.g., Harvard, Yale) mostly played other Eastern teams, Midwestern teams (e.g., Michigan, Wisconsin) other Midwestern teams. In the days of train travel, long-distance trips could take as much as a week, so intersectional games remained mostly a novelty. And the notion of crowning a national champion barely registered prior to the Associated Press publishing its now ubiquitous voter poll for the first time in 1936. Even then, the idea that amateur college students from scattered parts of the country would traverse great distances in December or January to determine whose team was the best seemed … preposterous. After Michigan and Notre Dame both finished the 1947 season undefeated, Wolverines coach Fitz Crisler dismissed suggestions the two should meet in a champion- ship game. Citing "weather, physical requirements and other factors," Crisler concluded, "It will just have to be a winter hot stove argument every year."

Watches For Everyone

Even with the advent of commercial airplanes, television and other societal developments that turned college sports into a nation- al enterprise, the resistance of the sports' leaders did not subside. By the 1950s the NCAA was shipping basketball teams around the country for its then 16-team tournament. Eight teams would convene in Omaha, Nebraska, for the six-day College World Series. But the bowl games – run by local community groups, not the NCAA – had developed a stranglehold on football's postseason. From 1936-1976, the number of bowls grew from just four to 12, as the celebratory events became one of the sport's most cherished traditions. In a more innocent time, there was no greater accomplishment for a college football team than reaching the Rose or Orange bowls. In fact, the AP conducted its final poll *before* the bowls all but one year prior to 1967; the coaches' poll did the same until 1973.

"Why do we need playoffs? Because the pros have them?" USC coach John McKay said after his team won the 1975 Liberty Bowl. "We have something better. We have eight or 10 teams who win their conferences, win bowl games, have great seasons. Ten winners instead of one. Everybody's happy. The alumni are happy. Recruiters are happy. They all say, 'We're No. 1.' The coach gets a raise. The players have a good time and get a new watch."

How do you argue with that?

But in fact, several of McKay's colleagues felt differently. In 1966, Michigan State coach Duffy Daugherty, whose team had split the mythical national championship the year before, suggested scrapping the New Year's Day bowls in favor of an eight-team playoff featuring six major conference champions and two independents. "The television revenue from an NCAA play-off would be tremendous," he said. "It would bring each school in the NCAA at least $20,000." Today, that amount would not even pay for one of Nick Saban's courtesy cars.

NCAA executive director Walter Byers endorsed Daugherty's idea … to a point. In a sentiment others would express many times over the ensuing five decades, Byers stipulated: "It would be critical that the very legitimate interests of the traditional friends on intercollegiate football, who through the years have conducted various bowl games, would be adequately protected." A nine-man NCAA committee, highlighted by Alabama coach Bear Bryant, began a playoff feasibility study in 1968 but disbanded within a year after garnering overwhelming backlash from both the major conferences and bowl representatives. "We've had several hundred letters," said WAC commissioner and committee chair Paul Brechler, "and they've varied in tone."

The playoff possibility came up again at the 1976 NCAA Convention in St. Louis, where 134 Division I schools were presented a proposal to select four of the New Year's Day bowl winners for a playoff. The authors needed only a simple majority vote for the concept to pass. Once again the bowls and major conferences opposed it, as did *Sports Illustrated*: "All the major bowls are the love objects of a handful of paid personnel and an army of volunteers, often men of high standing in the community," John Underwood wrote in a story about the impending vote. "… Take away the illusion of being No. 1 from any bowl and it will probably shrivel up." The bill never made it to the floor.

Various NCAA councils and subcommittees commissioned similarly ill-fated proposals in the 1980s and '90s. By then, Division I had split into two levels, Divisions I-A and I-AA (now referred to as FBS and FCS), with the NCAA staging a playoff for the smaller schools. But the major conferences (e.g., the Big Ten, the SEC) had ample incentive to keep the NCAA's hands out of their own postseason. In a largely unregulated market, the bowls made their payouts directly to the participating schools and conferences. The big boys had reason to fear an NCAA-sponsored event would cut into their take and force Auburn to share its Sugar Bowl check with Appalachian State. Meanwhile, from the earliest playoff movements, bowl folks made it abundantly clear they viewed any such proposal as a threat to the bowls' very existence. As such, bowl execs and volunteers in colored blazers devoted considerable money and effort over the years to wining and dining the school and conference officials who keep them in business. Therefore any effort to formalize the national championship process would have to find a way to incorporate the existing bowl games.

Let's Form an Alliance

Ironically, a bowl game that would one day get caught in a scandal involving its overzealous hospitality inadvertently spawned the first real momentum for an official championship. In 1986, the clear-cut top two teams in college football were a pair of independents, Miami and Penn State, neither of which were bound to a certain bowl game. These were the days when bowl organizers routinely cut deals with schools before the season even ended. In this case, the upstart Fiesta Bowl, founded just 15 years earlier, bet on the 'Canes and Nittany Lions remaining undefeated, which they did, setting up an epic primetime No. 1 vs. No. 2 clash. To that point, 1 vs. 2 match-ups in the bowls had been extremely rare – just eight in the AP poll's first 56 years – and largely accidental. But now the idea of formally pitting the top two teams in a bowl took hold.

In 1992, with conferences snapping up most of the major independents (Florida State to the ACC, Penn State to the Big Ten, Miami to the Big East), the ACC, Big East, Big 8, SEC, Southwest Conference and Notre Dame joined with the Orange, Sugar, Cotton and Fiesta bowls to form the Bowl Coalition, later rebranded the Bowl Alliance. The arrangement would free a No. 1 or 2 team among those leagues from its traditional partner bowl in order to stage a 1 vs. 2 game. From 1992-97 the Coalition/Alliance succeeded in staging three 1 vs. 2 matchups. Half the time, however, the absence of the Big Ten, Pac-10 and Rose Bowl prevented a true national championship game from taking place. The three parties had maintained an exclusive partnership since 1947 and adamantly opposed sharing that stage with others. Pasadena is an idyllic place where one might easily become detached from the outside world. Folks in charge didn't much care about the national champion. They just wanted to be left alone to enjoy New Year's. One prominent athletic director and playoff proponent often expressed frustration that the sport's national championship was "held hostage by the Rose Bowl Parade."

But in 1994, the Rose Bowl's autonomy deprived undefeated Big Ten champion Penn State from a chance at the national championship, which went instead to undefeated, top-ranked Nebraska. "It's a shame that the two best teams in the country didn't play each other," said Nittany Lions quarterback Kerry Collins. Wouldn't you know it, 18 months later, the commissioners of the other leagues – most notably the SEC's Roy Kramer – finally persuaded those remaining outliers to be part of a Super Alliance, subsequently rebranded as the Bowl Championship Series for its inaugural 1998 season.

Fifteen years later, the long-since retired Kramer recounted to AL.com just how skittish the Rose Bowl had been about possibly losing both of its traditional champs to another bowl. Kramer assured them that the Big Ten and Pac-10 champ had only finished Nos. 1

and 2 once in the previous 50 years. (It actually happened twice.) So of course, when the first-ever BCS standings came out on October 26, 1998, the No. 1 and 2 teams were … UCLA and Ohio State. "The Rose Bowl was about to walk out the door," said Kramer. "I said, 'If this happens, well, at least it won't happen for another 50 years.' That didn't go over very well." Mercifully, Tennessee and Florida State ended the season 1-2.

I'm going to assume nearly everyone reading this lived through at least part of the BCS era. No need to recount its entire checkered 16-year history. For all the criticism, the system largely achieved its initial intent. With the exception of one unfortunate aberration in 2003 it produced a consensus national champion every season. Interest in the sport's regular season skyrocketed as fans in one conference now cared intently about games in other conferences that affected the BCS championship race. "If you look at the growth of college football from '98 to [2013], it was pretty incredible," said Big Ten commissioner Jim Delany. "It separated itself out from the other sports and ended up as the No. 2 most popular sport in America. The BCS really grew and nationalized the sport."

But with increased attention came increased scrutiny. In 2003, Tulane president Scott Cowen organized a coalition of the lesser-regarded non-automatic qualifying conferences (e.g., Conference USA, the Mountain West) to demand a more egalitarian system. Congress held hearings. "The people that created the BCS created it with the idea that this was an end game," said SEC commissioner Mike Slive, "and other people saw it as the beginning of something new."

Other than adding a fifth bowl and loosening access requirements for the little guys in 2006 – which led to the BCS era's most enduring moment, Boise State's heart-stopping Fiesta Bowl upset of Oklahoma – the concept remained largely unchanged for 16 years. The most commonly trumpeted excuses ... er, explanations, for why expanding the field by two teams would be nothing short of disastrous included academic intrusions (but it's OK for FCS schools to play as many as four extra games); injury risk (apparently not of concern when approving a 12th regular season game in the mid-2000s); overcommercialization (ship sailed, fellas); and "bracket creep," a term invented by the BCS's highly-paid PR consultants – most notably former White House press secretary Ari Fleischer – to dramatize the slippery slope by which playoff fields inevitably expand from four to eight to 12 to 16 (that part will probably hold true).

Death to the BCS

The more the stewards defended their divisive system, the more criticism mounted. By 2010 the BCS was dealing with potential antitrust investigations by the Utah attorney general and the Department of Justice; IRS complaints filed by an upstart political action committee, Playoff PAC; and the scathing book *Death to the BCS* by Yahoo Sports columnist Dan Wetzel and two co-authors. The latter two groups directed much of their attention to the opulence of several bowl organizations, like the Orange Bowl's "Summer Splash," a three-day all-inclusive getaway to the Bahamas for athletic directors and commissioners. The never-ending playoff debate now included a cruise itinerary ("Dinner attire: resort casual") as fodder.

In 2011 the Fiesta Bowl delivered BCS critics their ultimate ammunition when an audit showed that longtime CEO John Junker, already in hot water for illegal campaign contributions (for which he was sentenced to six months in prison in 2014), had racked up myriad questionable expenses on the bowl's tab, including a $30,000 Pebble Beach birthday party and a $1,200 strip club visit. The Fiesta Bowl was allowed to remain a BCS bowl but made to pay a $1 million fine. Yet, as late as August of that year, the Big Ten's Delany insisted his league was "happy with the status quo."

And then, suddenly, it wasn't. Emerging from a meeting of the commissioners on January 8, 2012, in New Orleans, with negotiations for the next postseason contract set to begin that summer, Delany said of a four-team possibility: "Everything is in the mix. … The seven [BCS] founders are the six [major] conferences plus Notre Dame. Four years ago, five of us didn't want to have the conversation. Now, people want to have the conversation."

It was a landmark concession for a commissioner whose league, along with the Pac-12 and Rose Bowl, had long been viewed as the "Axis of Obstruction – as SI's Austin Murphy once wrote – in any play-off dialogue. The impossible finally seemed plausible. Just over five months later, Notre Dame AD Jack Swarbrick stood before reporters at a hastily arranged news conference in Chicago flanked by the FBS commissioners and proclaimed, "We have developed a consensus behind a four-team, seeded playoff." The presidents rubber-stamped their proposal six days later. As I wrote at the time, "Someone check the sky for pigs, the underworld for freezing temperatures."

To this day no one involved in the discussions has pinpointed a single impetus for the group's seemingly sudden about-face. "They are listening to the fans," BCS executive director Bill Hancock insisted that spring, minus an explanation why they'd tuned them out for

13 years before that. It's easy to point to that year's highly unpopular LSU-Alabama title game as the tipping point. Ironically, the one commissioner who'd championed a playoff the longest, the SEC's Slive, now needed it the least. His league was well into a dynasty that would eventually entail seven straight BCS championships, causing resentment and jealousy among his peers.

But the climate had begun shifting before then. For one thing, three of the six major conferences – the Big East, Big 12 and Pac-12 – changed commissioners between 2009 and 2011. All six added or lost schools in realignment mania. But mostly, the BCS's leaders grew tired of defending the thing. "There's a point at which university leadership says to you, 'Can you make this so I don't have to deal with this all the time?'" said Swarbrick. "'I'm really tired of hearing it in my mail and from trustees and from congressional representatives. I don't want to talk about this. I want to run my university.'"

The BCS couldn't die without one last round of territorial squabbling. Pac-12 commissioner Larry Scott, among others, pushed for a playoff consisting solely of conference champions. The SEC wasn't having that. The Big Ten initially proposed playing the semifinals on campus sites – much to the delight of the many deluded Midwesterners who believe their teams would win more bowl games if only the temperatures were colder – but found little support elsewhere. And the debate over how to pick the teams became like an interminable cable news show. Ultimately they opted for neutral sites, no restrictions on the participants and a selection committee to replace the BCS standings, a few of the many details I'll expound on in the coming pages. "It's gratifying," Slive said of his long-desired playoff finally coming to fruition. "It's taken 10 years."

Oh, and before you ask: "It's going to [stay at] four [teams] for 12 years," Hancock said in April 2014. "The [commissioners] did the four-team tournament because four is the number that doesn't erode the regular season and doesn't erode the bowl system. … We should embrace it and love it and treasure it and love to hear the words 'College Football Playoff.' Who'd have thunk it?"

Duffy Daugherty first thunk it nearly 50 years ago. Of course, he wanted eight teams. But hey, they're halfway there. Check back in another half century.

So There's a Playoff? When? Where?

The first thing to know about the College Football Playoff is that unlike the BCS, it is an actual organization. As I wrote in *Bowls, Polls and Tattered Souls*, "You cannot walk into some skyscraper in New York City or an office park in Topeka, Kansas, and ask to 'speak to someone with the BCS,' because the BCS does not physically exist."

Not so the College Football Playoff. In a 10th floor office suite in Las Colinas, Texas, a suburb outside Dallas, 13 full-time staff members hold meetings inside a conference room lined with logos of the 10 FBS conferences and make coffee in a break room decorated with helmets of the reigning league champions. Former Final Four director Bill Hancock, who became the first executive director of the BCS in 2009, retained his position with the CFP, while Michael Kelly, a former ACC associate commissioner, serves as the postseason's first chief operating officer. "We kind of pinch ourselves every day knowing we have a chance to be part of this great new iconic sporting event," said Kelly. We'll see if he still feels that way the first time the selection committee leaves out Alabama.

The new system certainly bears many resemblances to the old one. It includes guaranteed spots for the major conference champions and the continued involvement of the four former BCS bowls – Rose, Sugar, Orange and Fiesta. But the relationship between conferences and bowls is different in the new system. There are no longer "AQ" (automatic qualifier) and "non-AQ" conferences. Toss those from your vocabulary. Start familiarizing yourself instead with the concept of "contract bowls" and "contract conferences."

When the BCS reached death's doorstep two years ago, any bowl that hoped to be part of the playoff system was free to partner with any conference and vice versa. The Big Ten and Pac-12, as expected, renewed their longtime alliance with the Rose Bowl. The Big 12 and SEC decided to start their own primetime January 1 matchup in the Sugar Bowl. "A new January bowl tradition is born," SEC commissioner Mike Slive proclaimed before the conferences had even chosen which bowl would host their creation. And the ACC made a deal with the Orange Bowl, with the Big Ten, SEC and Notre Dame agreeing to rotate as that league's opponent. The realignment-ravaged Big East, now known as the American Athletic Conference, no longer enjoys the privileged status it did in the BCS. It tried to land its own contract bowl but found no takers. The commissioners of the Mountain West, Conference USA, MAC and Sun Belt are just happy they still get invited to the meetings.

So to recap, the Rose, Sugar and Orange are the three contract bowls. Each made its own 12-year deal with ESPN before the CFP was even formalized. The Rose's and Sugar's are valued at $80 million a year, the Orange's at $55 million. The CFP subsequently chose the Fiesta, Cotton and Peach (formerly known as the Chick-fil-A) to join those three as rotating hosts of its semifinal games; however, those other three bowls are not affiliated with any one conference. For the right to televise seven games a year – the national championship game, two semifinals and the four other major bowls – ESPN agreed to pay a staggering $7.3 billion over 12 years, according to *Sports Business Journal*. That's an annual average of $608 million, a 280 percent increase from its last BCS deal. A conference gets $4 million if one of its teams plays in the non-contract bowls (Fiesta, Cotton and Peach), $6 million for making one of the semifinals and nothing extra for the championship game. The CFP will cover $2 million in expenses for each participant.

All in all, nearly the entire pot, minus operating expenses, goes directly to the 10 FBS conferences and independents via the CFP – which in turn pays for new locker rooms with waterfalls in the teams' hydrotherapy pools. In this new arrangement, the bowls are essentially outside vendors to which CFP organizers will pay a fee to operate their games. "In the old era, those four [BCS] bowls paid a fee to be the hosts, but the spoils, or the margin, were maintained by that bowl," said Kelly. "In this case, that margin is maintained by us."

Easy as One, Two, Three

Major college football's first-ever pair of playoff semifinal games will be played January 1, 2015, at the Rose Bowl (5 p.m. eastern) and Sugar Bowl (8:30 p.m.). The first national championship game of the playoff era will be held Monday night, January 12, at AT&T Stadium in Arlington, Texas. Over the course of 12 seasons the semifinals will rotate among the six aforementioned bowls in three-year intervals. The Rose and Sugar host semifinal games in Year 1, the Orange and Cotton in Year 2 and the Fiesta and Peach in Year 3. Rinse and repeat.

The championship game, on the other hand, will not follow a predetermined rotation. So far, organizers have accepted bids only for the first three games. Glendale, Arizona, will host the second edition on January 11, 2016, Tampa the third on January 9, 2017. Officially, the sites are named North Texas, Arizona and Tampa Bay because multiple municipalities combined on each bid. If you're heading to the game, though, don't attempt to enter "North Texas" in your GPS, or you'll end up at a university in Denton. While the sites will fluctuate, the timing of the game will not. It will always be played on the first Monday night that falls at least seven days after the semifinals. The latest date over the 12-year cycle is January 13 (twice), the earliest January 7 (in 2019).

The six bowls involved in the playoff rotation – hereby known as "The New Year's Six" – will be played in a pair of tripleheaders on December 31 and January 1, though the January 1 bowls might occasionally slide to January 2 (as in 2017) to avoid a conflict with NFL Sundays.

Here is the rotation for the first three years:

2014-15

DATE	GAME	TEAM A	TEAM B
Dec. 31	Peach Bowl	At-large	At-large
Dec. 31	Fiesta Bowl	At-large	At-large
Dec. 31	Orange Bowl	ACC	SEC/B1G/ND
Jan. 1	Cotton Bowl	At-large	At-large
Jan. 1	**Rose Bowl**	**Semifinal team**	**Semifinal team**
Jan. 1	**Sugar Bowl**	**Semifinal team**	**Semifinal team**
Jan. 12	National Championship	Rose Bowl winner	Sugar Bowl winner

2015-16

DATE	GAME	TEAM A	TEAM B
Dec. 31	Peach Bowl	At-large	At-large
Dec. 31	**Orange Bowl**	**Semifinal team**	**Semifinal team**
Dec. 31	**Cotton Bowl**	**Semifinal team**	**Semifinal team**
Jan. 1	Fiesta Bowl	At-large	At-large
Jan. 1	Rose Bowl	Big Ten	Pac-12
Jan. 1	Sugar Bowl	Big 12	SEC
Jan. 11	National Championship	Orange Bowl winner	Cotton Bowl winner

2016-17

DATE	GAME	TEAM A	TEAM B
Dec. 31	Orange Bowl	ACC	SEC/B1G/ND
Dec. 31	**Peach Bowl**	**Semifinal team**	**Semifinal team**
Dec. 31	**Fiesta Bowl**	**Semifinal team**	**Semifinal team**
Jan. 2	Cotton Bowl	At-large	At-large
Jan. 2	Rose Bowl	Big Ten	Pac-12
Jan. 2	Sugar Bowl	Big 12	SEC
Jan. 9	National Championship	Peach Bowl winner	Fiesta Bowl winner

As you may notice, two out of every three years, the semifinal games will take place on New Year's Eve, not New Year's Day. That's because the Rose and Sugar locked in their January 1 time slots with ESPN before officials finalized the larger playoff rotation, and because the commissioners wanted to keep the two semifinals on the same day so neither winner gets an extra day to prepare for the title game.

This new wrinkle in the football calendar could either be really awesome or really polarizing, depending on whether a football fan is, say, married to a non-football fan accustomed to a romantic evening on December 31. The playoff "has a chance to redefine the country's perspective of what the New Year's holiday means to people and how people plan out their personal lives over those two days," ESPN's chief college football programming executive Burke Magnus told AL.com.

Organizers envision New Year's Eve becoming a de facto Super Bowl Sunday. "It will absolutely change the paradigm of New Year's Eve in this country," said Hancock. "[People] want to go to New Year's Eve parties, but they're going to know those parties are going to have a television set where people are watching college football."

It's an ambitious goal, though the bigger issue might not be New Year's Eve itself but the afternoon of New Year's Eve. Depending on the day of the week, December 31 is a regular workday for many people, and the first of the two games will kick off no later than 5 p.m. eastern time – 2 p.m. on the West Coast. It's a big gamble by organizers who are anticipating TV audiences for the two semifinal games eventually exceeding those of the BCS championship game, which drew 26 million viewers for the 2014 Florida State-Auburn matchup. It remains to be seen whether ratings for that early game will suffer initially. More likely, December 31 will soon become its own holiday.

In order to further establish December 31 as a Really Big Deal, the networks have moved all other bowls, like recent mainstays the

Sun Bowl and Liberty Bowl, to earlier dates. The Capital One and Outback remain on January 1 but the Gator Bowl has moved to January 2. "The six [biggest] games will be packaged together very tightly," said Magnus.

A Tradition Like No Other ... Two Out of Three Years

While the commissioners were adamant about protecting the bowls in a playoff system, one out of every three years they'll lose a bit of their traditional identity. The official names of the first semifinal bowls will be the College Football Playoff at the Rose Bowl and the College Football Playoff at the Sugar Bowl. Really rolls off the tongue, no? And technically, the game in Pasadena is the College Football Playoff at the Rose Bowl presented by Northwestern Mutual. Good luck, T-shirt designers. When the ESPN broadcast begins and the cameras pan the stadium, "the imagery will be a prominent playoff symbol at midfield," said Kelly. "The iconic Rose Bowl [logo] will be on the field as well. But the dominant brand will be the Playoff."

If by chance a football fan emerges from a seven-year slumber on January 1, turns on the television at 5 p.m. EST and sees Georgia and Baylor playing each other in something called the College Football Playoff at the Rose Bowl, he might naturally wonder, "When's the real Rose Bowl?" And the answer is: They're one and the same.

Once every three years, when its turn in the playoff rotation comes up, the Rose Bowl will not host its traditional Big Ten-Pac-12 matchup. Ditto the Sugar Bowl's new SEC-Big 12 pairing and, in 2015-16, the Orange Bowl's ACC game. If a champion from one of those contract conferences doesn't make the playoff and finds its traditional bowl occupied by semifinal imposters, it's guaranteed a spot in one of the three open bowls. So if, say, UCLA wins the Pac-12 in 2014 but isn't ranked in the selection committee's top four, the Bruins will not go to the Rose Bowl; they'll be placed instead in the Fiesta, Cotton or Peach. Cheer up, UCLA fans. That still beats another trip to El Paso.

Obviously, the Rose Bowl is not thrilled with this arrangement, but what choice did it have? Theoretically it could have bowed out of the playoff group altogether and hosted a Big Ten-Pac-12 game every year for eternity, but the Granddaddy would lose considerable prestige. "The Rose Bowl recognized that the world is changing," said Oregon State president Ed Ray. Besides, such deviations from tradition are not unprecedented. Five times in the BCS era, the Pasadena game hosted teams from other conferences, including the Miami-Nebraska (2002) and Texas-USC (2006) national championship games (before the BCS went to a standalone title game) as well as TCU's historic appearance in 2011 while then a member of the Mountain West.

Additionally, unlike in the old system, the game is 100 percent guaranteed to be Big Ten vs. Pac-12 two of every three years. If No. 3 Ohio State goes to the playoff and the next highest-ranked Big Ten team is No. 22 Michigan State, so be it. The Spartans go to Pasadena. By the same token, if the Sugar Bowl loses No. 1 Florida to the playoff and is not hosting a semifinal, it will take the next highest-ranked SEC team regardless of its ranking. It cannot bypass No. 5 Missouri for No. 13 LSU just because the in-state team might buy more tickets. The contract bowls' contracts are with their partner conferences, not the CFP, giving those parties the necessary autonomy to avoid another TCU trip to Pasadena. (Unless, of course, the Rose Bowl is a playoff game and TCU makes the playoff.)

It's up to the selection committee which playoff teams go to which semifinal bowl, but both Hancock and committee chairman Jeff Long said it will come down to which of the two sites is more sensible geographically for the No. 1 seed. "The committee picks, but No. 1 gets the preference," said Hancock. Notice that all three semifinal pairings, Rose-Sugar, Orange-Cotton and Fiesta-Peach, involve both an east and west – or at least central – location. If, as in 2013, Florida State is No. 1 and Auburn is No. 2, both would presumably prefer New Orleans to Pasadena. As the higher-ranked team, FSU would get first dibs on the Big Easy, with Auburn shipped west. If it's the 2015 season, when the Cotton and Orange bowls take their playoff-hosting turns, and if Oregon is No. 1 and Oklahoma No. 2, Oregon would get the Cotton and Oklahoma the Orange even though Norman, Okla., is just three hours from Arlington. As their reward for earning the No. 1 seed the Ducks won't get sent 3,300 miles away just for Sooners fans' convenience.

The only wiggle room may come if the natural order results in a lower-seeded team getting home-field advantage. Suppose the matchups in 2014 are No. 1 Alabama-No. 4 Clemson and

No. 2 Texas A&M-No. 3 UCLA. Alabama would get first dibs on the Sugar Bowl, but that would leave A&M playing a true road game at the Rose Bowl. The committee might then opt to put Alabama-Clemson in Pasadena and A&M-UCLA in New Orleans, but so far there's no formal mandate, and officials have been vague about the possibility. Should one of those scenarios arise, I'm sure fans of the teams involved will be happy with whatever the committee decides. I'll wait a minute for you stop laughing.

Even as playoff games, the host bowls will still feel like traditional bowl games for the teams themselves. "We're planning to have the playoff semifinal weeks be very similar to what the BCS championship weeks were like," said Kelly. "It will be a six-night stay. It will be the quote-unquote bowl experience for the coaches and student-athletes." In other words, the Disneyland visit and the Lawry's Beef Bowl will remain on the Rose Bowl's pregame itinerary, albeit early in the week.

The new national championship game, on the other hand, will be an entirely new experience for college football.

If You Build It, Will They Come?

The BCS went to a double-hosting model (two games in one city) for its title game in 2007, and the eight subsequent editions occurred anywhere from January 6 to January 10. So the later date is not new. However, the teams in those games had not played in a bowl game 10 days earlier as the playoff finalists will. More to the point: The BCS

National Championship Game was itself a bowl game. The College Football Playoff National Championship is not.

As the NFL does with the Super Bowl or the NCAA with the Final Four, the CFP bid out the championship sites to any interested city. Would you like to host the national championship game? Just provide at least a 65,000-seat stadium, 15,000 suitable hotel rooms and meet a few other requirements. While the same people who run the Cotton Bowl were part of the Local Organizing Committee that engineered Dallas/Arlington's successful bid for the inaugural game, it is not by any means a Cotton Bowl. Kelly and his team are primarily running the game, and they envision it becoming a more grandiose coronation than any the sport has ever seen. "It will start off as a hybrid" of the Final Four and Super Bowl, said Kelly. "We're kind of blessed to have iconic status from the beginning just because of what the BCS championship game became, but we want to expand on that."

Unlike the semifinals, the final will not involve a traditional bowl week. Following a week of practice back home, teams will arrive by Friday night, participate in a Media Day on Saturday, hold their walk-throughs on Sunday and play the game Monday night. Meanwhile, the Dallas/Fort Worth Metroplex will host a raging party. Planned activities include a weekend-long FanFest and multi-day music festival. And unlike the Super Bowl, in which a swarm of B- and C-list celebrities, corporate shills and other assorted hangers-on flood the town for the parties, then leave before the game, CFP organizers envision a more mainstream crowd. "It will not be a junior Super Bowl. We don't gain by being compared to the Super Bowl," said

Hancock. "It's a college event. We're going to have 40,000 fans of Auburn and Florida State in town to celebrate their team and celebrate the game."

But is that a realistic projection? And if it is, should the Rose and Sugar Bowls be worried?

One of the biggest concerns initially about keeping the playoff within the bowl system – and as such, one of the arguments initially for holding the semifinals on campus sites – was whether it's reasonable to expect fans of a contending team to travel to both a January 1 bowl and the January 12 championship game. "In the bowl system they have a month to prepare, figure out a way to get there," Mountain West commissioner Craig Thompson said during the 2012 discussions. "It will be extremely challenging to move large sections of fans [twice]." Not to mention costly. Have you ever tried to book a cross-country flight less than 14 days in advance? Are you familiar with four-night hotel minimums? Furthermore, among the power conferences, all but the Big 12 now play a championship game at neutral sites. That's three round-trips in less than six weeks – not to mention the increasingly popular season-opening neutral site "classics."

In 2014, defending national champion Florida State opens the season against Oklahoma State in the Cowboys Classic in Arlington – same site as the national title game four months later. If the 'Noles win the ACC Atlantic Division, they'll play in the conference title game in Charlotte. If they finish in the top four, they'll head to a Playoff semifinal game. Let's say it's in Pasadena. Win that and they return to North Texas. According to Expedia, the combined lowest air fares from Tallahassee for a pair of 'Noles fans hoping to follow their team to all four games is $4,048. For average-priced hotels in all four cities – two nights for the regular-season games, three nights for the playoff games – add another $1,865. And who knows how many more thousands the actual game tickets will cost. Face value for the title game starts at $450. The good news: If the 'Noles win it all, that couple will have memories for a lifetime. The bad news: They can no longer afford to send their kids to FSU, or any other college for that matter.

Chances are, the conference title games will actually suffer the most in attendance if fans feel confident their team is heading to the playoff. At least the semifinals have the advantage of falling on a holiday. "Ticket prices are going to be reasonable for the semifinals for the schools and we're going to do everything possible to make the semifinals as regional as possible," said Hancock.

Getting to Dallas on a Monday night less than two weeks later may be a taller order. Pac-12 commissioner Larry Scott admits there's no way to predict how the extra round will affect fan travel. But he's optimistic. "I don't know that any of our schools' [fan bases] are going take it for granted that if they make it to the semifinals, they're going to win that game and go to the championship game, or that they'll go another year," said Scott. "I think this is going to be so special to make the playoff, fans are going to rally and they're going both to the semifinal games and the championship game."

Mind you, the CFP folks don't necessarily need the *same* 40,000 Florida State or Auburn fans to attend both games. According to a 2011 study by noted statistician Nate Silver, then with the *New York Times*, Auburn has 1.9 million fans scattered across the country,

Florida State about 813,000. The nation's most popular team per his data, Ohio State, has more than 3 million. Those numbers seem high, but Ohio State does have an estimated 500,000 living alumni. Organizers only need a small fraction of that pool to fill the stands, not to mention the fact fans in the cities hosting the games may be more motivated to attend a playoff or championship game than a traditional bowl game.

College football fans are incredibly passionate. Here's guessing that between the novelty of the playoff and the increased magnitude of the semifinal bowls, organizers will have little trouble filling seats in either round for at least the first few years. Even if they don't, they still get their $7.3 billion in ESPN money. Furthermore, the playoff will have a larger effect on the sport's overall popularity. Granted, it's already doing pretty well for itself. In an annual poll conducted by Harris Interactive, college football has closed a once sizeable gap behind Major League Baseball as the nation's second most popular sport behind the NFL. Still, there's always been a contingent of the fan population – particularly on the East Coast and in big cities where the NFL reigns supreme – for whom the convoluted BCS has failed to resonate. But almost everybody loves and understands a bracket. "If this does as much as the BCS did for the growth of college football, we'll be fortunate," said Delany. "There's still a lot of growth left in the sport and what we've been able to do is take the next step in an evolutionary way."

So go ahead and mark your calendar for the 2015 Rose Bowl. It's the same date, same time, same stadium – but with a new name, new midfield logo and considerably bigger stakes.

What About the Other Bowls?

On the last day of the 2011 season, Southern Miss upset undefeated Houston in the Conference USA championship game, ending the Kevin Sumlin-coached Cougars' hopes of an at-large berth in a BCS bowl. The Sugar Bowl now had two spots to fill. Michigan, 10-2, was a surefire bet for one of them. The Wolverines, with their large national following, had not been to a BCS bowl in five years. For their opponent, the New Orleans game had at least two appealing choices – Boise State, 11-1 and playing its last game with standout quarterback Kellen Moore, and 10-2 Kansas State, its rabid fan base eager to celebrate a surprising turnaround season.

Yet come Selection Sunday, the folks in New Orleans made the head-scratching decision to take ... Virginia Tech, 11-2 and ranked 17th in the AP poll following a 38-10 loss to Clemson in the previous night's ACC championship game. Even Hokies fans didn't seem particularly enthusiastic. Asked about his bowl's rationale, CEO Paul Hoolahan cited ... well, cronyism. The Hokies had been to his game twice in the 2000s; the other two had never been. Their coach, Frank Beamer, had been "a very good friend throughout the years," said Hoolahan. Kansas State AD John Currie later lamented to CBSSports.com: "If we want to have five [BCS bowl] games which we determine – because of the tag we put on them – as being the best five, then we might be at the point where we need to take more objective criteria into account."

Three years later – wish granted!

College football fans have long conditioned themselves to an often-maddening rite of early December in which the major bowls select their teams based primarily on who will sell the most tickets and fill the most hotel rooms or whose coach or AD is particularly chummy with the bowl director. But in the College Football Playoff era, even the non-playoff participants among the so-called New Year's Six (Rose, Sugar, Orange, Fiesta, Cotton and Peach) will be decided by – brace yourself – merit. "The bowls won't have any input because they don't really need to have input," said Hancock. "The job of the bowl team selection chairman is obsolete. Gone."

If you remember just one nugget from this entire book, I hope it will be this: The new Playoff selection committee is not just picking the top four teams. Let me repeat: *The selection committee is not just picking the top four teams.* Its rankings will be used to determine the participants in all six major bowls. And the committee, not the bowls themselves, will create the respective matchups.

Now, don't take that to mean that the New Year's Six will consist solely of the Top 12 teams in the country. That would be far too simple and fan-friendly, and this is still a system controlled by the major conferences. Various contractual obligations must be met first when placing the teams in the bowls; in fact, there may be instances when a lowly ranked or even unranked team that never would have qualified for the more restrictive BCS gets into one of these games. However, there shouldn't be any surprises like 2011 Virginia Tech once everybody gets familiar with the new arrangement. The selection process is entirely objective, albeit overly complicated:

• First, the top four teams are placed in the two semifinal bowls. As discussed in the last chapter, those sites are predetermined on a rotating basis.

• The champions of the five conferences with contract bowls – the Big Ten and Pac-12 (Rose), the SEC and Big 12 (Sugar) and the ACC (Orange) – are guaranteed a spot if they don't reach the playoff. If their partner bowl is available, they automatically go there. If their partner bowl is hosting a semifinal, they'll go to either the Cotton, Fiesta or Peach bowls, none of which have designated conference tie-ins.

• If the Rose, Sugar or Orange is not hosting a semifinal and loses its contracted conference champion to the playoff, then it will get the committee's next highest-ranked team from that conference. Unlike the old system, where said team still needed to finish in the Top 14 to qualify, there are no required minimums in those three bowls' contracts. If the Orange Bowl loses No. 1 Florida State to the playoff and No. 22 Georgia Tech is the ACC's next highest-ranked team, then Georgia Tech it is. But trust me, it's a more merit-based system. Keep reading.

• The committee's highest-ranked champion from among the five other conferences – American, Conference USA, MAC, Mountain West and Sun Belt – is also guaranteed a spot in the Cotton, Fiesta or Peach bowls. This is a notable difference from the BCS, where a non-AQ champ had to be ranked either in the Top 12 or the Top 16 if ranked above one of the AQ champs. In both 2011 and 2013, for example, no such team qualified. Now there will be one every year, no matter the ranking. "Conference USA is delighted about it," said that league's commissioner, Britton Banowsky.

Merit. It's coming.

• If the Orange Bowl is not hosting a semifinal, then the committee's rankings will be used in part to determine the ACC's opponent. This is where things get particularly complicated. The Big Ten, SEC and Notre Dame have a shared deal with the Orange Bowl, which gets the committee's highest-ranked available team from that group. But there are stipulations. For one, that team cannot be the Big Ten's or SEC's champion, only an at-large team. Additionally, the Big Ten and SEC are each guaranteed at least three appearances over the course of 12 years while Notre Dame will get a maximum of two. This pick should be pretty straightforward the first few years but could get tricky by, say, 2021.

• Now … ready for it? The highest-ranked available teams still left on the committee's board will fill any remaining at-large spots among the six bowls. That number will vary from year to year based on which bowls are hosting the semifinals and which conferences make the playoff. Some years there could be four open spots; some years there may only be one. But if Boise State is No. 7, Ohio State is No. 8 and there's only one spot left in any of the six bowls, the committee can't bypass the Broncos for the Buckeyes.

Ohio State fans will undoubtedly blame the slight on oversigning.

Fun With Hypotheticals

To better conceptualize the new process, let's do a mock selection based on the 2013 season. For simplicity's sake we'll assume the committee's rankings are the same as the final BCS standings, which were as follows:

1	Florida State	13-0	ACC champ
2	Auburn	12-1	SEC champ
3	Alabama	11-1	
4	Michigan State	12-1	Big Ten champ
5	Stanford	11-2	Pac-12 champ
6	Baylor	11-1	Big 12 champ
7	Ohio State	12-1	
8	Missouri	11-2	
9	South Carolina	10-2	
10	Oregon	10-2	
11	Oklahoma	10-2	
12	Clemson	10-2	
13	Oklahoma State	10-2	
14	Arizona State	10-3	
15	UCF	11-1	American champ

Now let's place the teams based on the 2014-15 bowl lineup, in which the Rose and Sugar are semifinal hosts:

• Florida State, Auburn, Alabama and Michigan State are playoff-bound.

• Pac-12 champ Stanford, displaced from the Rose Bowl, is guaranteed a spot elsewhere. Ditto Big 12 champ Baylor, displaced from the Sugar Bowl.

• Since the Orange Bowl lost ACC champ FSU to the playoff it gets the next highest-ranked ACC team, in this case No. 12 Clemson. The Tigers' opponent would be the highest-ranked available team from among the SEC, Big Ten or Notre Dame. In this case that's No. 7 Ohio State.

• No. 15 UCF, as the highest-ranked champ from the other five conferences, is guaranteed a spot as well.

• The aforementioned teams account for nine of the 12 berths in the New Year's Six bowls, so the committee tabs the three highest-ranked teams left on its board to fill the remaining spots. They are No. 8 Missouri, No. 9 South Carolina and No. 10 Oregon.

Thus, the three contract bowls are No. 1 Florida State-No. 4 Michigan State in the Sugar semifinal (due to top seed FSU's proximity to New Orleans), No. 2 Auburn-No. 3 Alabama in the Rose semifinal (heaven help us all) and No. 7 Ohio State-No. 12 Clemson in the Orange (as actually happened in 2013). We won't know until they do it for real how exactly the committee will decide who plays where between the Cotton, Fiesta and Peach. But according to an October 2013 news release:

The committee will use geography as a consideration in the pairing of teams and assigning them to bowl sites ... The committee will attempt to avoid regular-season rematches when assigning teams to these non-playoff bowl games. ... To benefit fans and student-athletes, the committee will attempt to avoid assigning a particular team or group of teams to the same bowl game repeatedly. Conference championships will be a criteria to be considered when the commit-tee assigns teams to bowls (i.e., if Dallas were a convenient site for two teams, preference would go to a conference champion).

Given those parameters, I came up with the following bowl lineup:

Dec. 31 Peach: No. 8 Missouri (at-large) vs. No. 15 UCF (non-contract champ)

Dec. 31 Fiesta: No. 5 Stanford (Pac-12 champ) vs. No. 9 South Carolina (at-large)

Dec. 31 Orange: No. 7 Ohio State (B1G/SEC/ND) vs. No. 12 Clemson (ACC)

Jan. 1 Cotton: No. 6 Baylor (Big 12 champ) vs. No. 10 Oregon (at-large)

Jan. 1 Rose: No. 2 Auburn (SEC champ) vs. No. 3 Alabama (at-large)

Jan. 1 Sugar: No. 1 FSU (ACC champ) vs. No. 4 Michigan State (B1G champ)

As conference champs, Baylor (in Texas) and Stanford (in Arizona) got geographic preference. Oregon to the Cotton made geographic sense and allowed for a must-see matchup between explosive, hur-ry-up offenses. I would have liked to place South Carolina in nearby Atlanta, but that would have caused a rematch with regular-season opponent UCF – unless I shipped UCF to Arizona, but then the highest-ranked non-playoff team, Stanford, would get the lowest-ranked opponent. So I sent the Gamecocks to face the Cardinal, leaving Missouri and UCF in the Peach. The Atlanta game, like Jacksonville Jaguars fans, would get Blake Bortles instead of Johnny Manziel.

Now let's mix it up. Same teams, same rankings but pretend this is 2016-17, when the semifinal sites are the Peach and Fiesta. Notice how much the lineup changes.

Dec. 31 Orange: No. 9 South Carolina (SEC/B1G/ND) vs. No. 12 Clemson (ACC)

Dec. 31 Peach: No. 1 FSU (ACC champ) vs. No. 4 Michigan State (B1G champ)

Dec. 31 Fiesta: No. 2 Auburn (SEC champ) vs. No. 3 Alabama (at-large)

Jan. 2 Cotton: No. 10 Oregon (at-large) vs. No. 15 UCF (at-large)

Jan. 2 Rose: No. 5 Stanford (Pac-12 champ) vs. No. 7 Ohio State (B1G)

Jan. 2 Sugar: No. 6 Baylor (Big 12 champ) vs. No. 8 Missouri (SEC)

In this scenario, Stanford, Ohio State, Baylor and Missouri all get to go to their conference's contract bowls and South Carolina goes to the Orange Bowl as the highest-ranked available team from among the SEC, Big Ten and Notre Dame. Unfortunately, that creates an Orange Bowl rematch between rivals South Carolina and Clemson, which just played each other in their last game. Since both the Sugar and Orange have contracts with the SEC, it's possible the parties could swap Missouri and South Carolina, but for now, we're following the letter of the law.

Simply by switching up which bowls hosted the semifinals, only one bowl, the Cotton, ended up without locked-in teams, as opposed to three in the 2014-15 lineup. That left Oregon and UCF as the default participants. Here's a strange but true quirk to the semifinal rotation: Once every three years, like this one, the Cotton will have to take the designated non-power conference champ because there's no other opening for that team. That wrinkle was not intentional, and the Cotton seems fine with it for now, but then again it's just grateful to be back among the elite tier of bowls after nearly two decades in purgatory. We'll see how they feel after one too many trips from Northern Illinois.

Clearance Sale on Bowl Tickets

Yet again, we see the diminished autonomy of bowl games in the new system. Emboldened in part by the *Death to the BCS*-inspired backlash against the perceived excesses of bowl organizers, the conferences took more control of their postseason arrangements. For example, the age-old practice of requiring participating schools to purchase a certain number of tickets has proved incredibly inefficient in the era of StubHub and Craigslist. Fans aren't going to buy full-priced seats through their school's official allocation if there are cheaper options available. The Orange Bowl in particular has seen its tickets sold for as low as 99 cents apiece on sites like eBay. A quick search turned up a copy of MC Hammer's "Too Legit to Quit" going for the same price. Stories circulate annually about schools losing money due to unsold ticket blocks – like Connecticut's losing $1.8 million on the 2011 Fiesta Bowl, an extreme example. But bowls rely heavily on those locked-in ticket sales to avoid taking a bath in years when their game might not be particularly attractive.

Ticket guarantees aren't going away, but the conferences did get the New Year's Six to reduce their requirements to 12,500 per school, down from 17,500 for the BCS bowls (not including the Rose). "The number of bowls grew and the fan bases got overexposed to certain regions. The demand fell for the tickets," said Big Ten commissioner Jim Delany. "We just felt it was out of balance. What are we taking all these tickets for?"

How drastically has the bowls' gravy train derailed? In March 2014 the Fiesta Bowl laid off more than half of its 33 employees, citing decreased revenue in the new system due to the CFP's, not the bowls', running the new championship game. "We don't have the revenue pieces we used to have," Duane Woods, the bowl's interim executive director, told the *Arizona Republic*. "It's a whole different landscape than in the past." Sources familiar with the contracts said the drop-off is not as dire as Woods paints it but does put an onus on the bowls to sell more tickets themselves.

The budding power shift between conferences and bowls is also trickling down to some leagues' arrangements with their lower-profile bowls. In the past, a conference's partner bowls chose their participants in a predetermined selection order based primarily on their respective payouts and prestige. While there were some restrictions on the process – for example, a clause preventing a bowl from bypassing a 10-2 team in favor of an 8-4 team – the bowls mostly chose based on their own nebulous criteria like fan following and how a team finished its season. This in turn gave bowl volunteers in their gaudy red or yellow blazers an excuse to score press passes at games around the country under the auspices of "scouting" possible participants. Because you just know the Gator Bowl decided between Nebraska and Minnesota based on whether that 66-year-old optometrist on its board enjoyed his free trip to Lincoln.

In an effort to produce more sensible matchups and avoid schools making too many repeat trips to the same bowl, the ACC, Big Ten and SEC are all employing a less rigid selection order in the new cycle by pooling together groups of similarly tiered bowls. Come the end of the season, the leagues will work "in consultation with the schools and the bowl games" to figure out the right team for each game, per the SEC. Translation: Mike Slive will pick. "If someone's going to the same bowl for a third year in a row, we're probably going to frown on it," said the Big Ten's Delany. "We have taken on that responsibility to be influential [in placing teams]. We'll probably get some heat for it."

To better understand how this approach differs from in the past, let's compare the Big Ten's 2013 bowl lineup, which followed a straightforward 1 through 8 selection process, and its 2014-19 lineup, which, in addition to featuring several new destinations, pools bowls 2 through 9 into a three-tiered system. Note: In the 2014-19 column, "College Football Playoff" includes any teams selected for the Rose, Orange or other New Year's Six bowls. Also, the Little Caesars Bowl is gone but replaced by a new Detroit game, while the 68-year-old Gator Bowl is now called the TaxSlayer Bowl. Someone's got to keep the lights on.

BIG TEN BOWLS, 2013

1	BCS
2	Capital One
3	Outback
4	Buffalo Wild Wings
5	Gator
6	Texas
7	Heart of Dallas
8	Little Caesars

BIG TEN BOWLS, 2014-19

1	College Football Playoff
2-4	Capital One
2-4	Outback
2-4	Holiday
5-7	TaxSlayer or Music City
5-7	San Francisco
5-7	Pinstripe
8-9	Heart of Dallas or Armed Forces
8-9	Detroit

In addition to employing a pool system, the Big Ten has also mandated that all of the bowls with six-year deals will feature at least five different teams over that span; the Pinstripe Bowl, which has an eight-year deal, will host at least six different teams. "If youre going to do a six-year, eight-year deal, you need to be able to move teams around," said Delany. In theory, all of these moves should keep the bowl pairings fresh and give fans opportunities to visit a variety of cities – while also making it virtually impossible for writers like me to author our late-season bowl projections columns with any semblance of accuracy.

No Such Thing as Too Much Football

Even the less powerful conferences have taken more control of their postseason opportunities – albeit not necessarily by choice. When the American Athletic Conference went shopping for partners in the 2014-19 cycle, it found out that a conference with Memphis instead of Louisville and SMU instead of Syracuse was not nearly as attractive to the Florida bowls. So the league started its own, the Miami Beach Bowl, to be played at Marlins Park. The conference itself owns and administers the game, and its opponent the first year will be independent BYU.

That game is one of four new bowls joining the landscape in 2014, along with the Bahamas Bowl (you'll need a passport with your game ticket), the Boca Raton Bowl (to be squeezed in between residents' Bocce ball and shuffleboard games) and the Camellia Bowl in Montgomery, Alabama. (A camellia is the Alabama state flower, which surprised me when I found that out. I'd assumed the state flower resided in Nick Saban's backyard.) All pit some combination of the American, Conference USA, MAC and Sun Belt. Yet another game, the Cure Bowl in Orlando, will join the fray in 2015, at which point the system will comprise 39 bowls and the national championship game.

In the meantime, in 2014, 59.3 percent of FBS teams – 76 out of 128 – will participate in a bowl. YOU get a trophy. … And YOU get a trophy …

My own opinion about the "too many bowls" topic has changed over the years. In *Bowls, Polls and Tattered Souls* I actually suggested cutting the number of bowls in half – and that was with the lineup at a more modest 32 games. The increasing prevalence of 6-6 teams, some of which may have even gone 2-6 in their own conference, had devalued the larger bowl system. "There's no doubt about it – the more bowls, the more exposure, it's not as special as it once was," said Delany. "You want to be special, and yet if you have too many games, the specialness of the bowl experience wears off."

But really, who is the Camellia Bowl hurting? The coaches and players get another three weeks together (save for the coaches who leave for a new job and the players who transfer between semesters), the fans get to watch their teams one more time and we all get more football. Lest you have any doubt about the power of televised college football on a weeknight in December, know that even ESPN's lowest-rated bowls still outdraw nearly all of its other non-football sporting events. For example, in 2013, the December 27 Syracuse-Minnesota Texas Bowl drew a higher rating (2.5) than the Syracuse-Louisville Big East basketball tournament final (2.1) earlier that year. All but five of that year's 35 bowls drew a higher rating than the network's 1.3 average for *Sunday Night Baseball*. So of course when the MAC or Sun Belt approached ESPN about starting even more bowl games, the network was all too eager to write the check. ESPN now airs 38 of 39 postseason games and owns and operates 10 of them. "We have a huge investment in the bowl business broadly," said ESPN's Burke Magnus. "We want to make sure the entire bowl enterprise is healthy."

Given that nearly every major conference has added and/or lost certain partner bowls and in some cases changed their selection process, here's a friendly conference-by-conference guide to each of the Power 5's 2014-19 lineup.

ACC (which includes Notre Dame)

	BOWL	CITY	OPPONENT
1	Orange/College Football Playoff		
2	Russell Athletic	Orlando	Big 12
3-6	Sun	El Paso, Texas	Pac-12
3-6	Belk	Charlotte	SEC
3-6	Music City or TaxSlayer	Nashville/Jacksonville	SEC
3-6	Pinstripe	New York	Big Ten
7-9	Military	Annapolis, Md.	American
7-9	Independence	Shreveport, La.	SEC
7-9	Detroit	Detroit	Big Ten
10	St. Petersburg (2014 & '16)	St. Petersburg, Fla.	American

The ACC will also take the Big Ten's spot in the Capital One Bowl in years when the Big Ten places a team in the Orange Bowl. When that happens, Capital One will select after Russell Athletic.

Big Ten

	BOWL	CITY	OPPONENT
1	Rose/College Football Playoff		
2-4	Capital One	Orlando	SEC
2-4	Outback	Tampa	SEC
2-4	Holiday	San Diego	Pac-12
5-7	TaxSlayer or Music City	Jacksonville/Nashville	SEC
5-7	San Francisco	Santa Clara, Calif.	Pac-12
5-7	Pinstripe	New York	ACC
8-9	Heart of Dallas or Armed Forces	Dallas/Fort Worth	C-USA/American
8-9	Detroit	Detroit	ACC

Big 12

	BOWL	CITY	OPPONENT
1	Sugar/College Football Playoff		
2	Alamo	San Antonio	Pac-12
3	Russell Athletic	Orlando	ACC
4	Texas	Houston	SEC
5	Liberty	Memphis	SEC
6	Buffalo Wild Wings	Tempe, Ariz.	Pac-12
7	Heart of Dallas or Armed Forces	Dallas/Fort Worth	C-USA/American

Pac-12

	BOWL	CITY	OPPONENT
1	Rose/College Football Playoff		
2	Alamo	San Antonio	Big 12
3	Holiday	San Diego	Big Ten
4	San Francisco	Santa Clara, Calif.	Big Ten

5	Sun	El Paso, Texas	ACC
6	Las Vegas	Las Vegas	Mountain West
7	Buffalo Wild Wings	Tempe, Ariz.	Big 12

SEC

	BOWL	CITY	OPPONENT
1	Sugar/College Football Playoff		
2	Capital One	Orlando	Big Ten
3-8	Outback	Tampa	Big Ten
3-8	TaxSlayer	Jacksonville, Fla.	Big Ten or ACC
3-8	Music City	Nashville	Big Ten or ACC
3-8	Liberty	Memphis	Big 12
3-8	Texas	Houston	Big 12
3-8	Belk	Charlotte	ACC
9	Birmingham	Birmingham, Ala.	American
10	Independence	Shreveport, La.	ACC

Bowls have unquestionably lost much of their cachet over the years, and it will be interesting to see how the College Football Playoff affects their business. After all, as discussed in an earlier chapter, the primary reason it took so many decades for the sport to adopt even a modest postseason tourney was the widespread belief that a playoff would eventually render the bowls extinct. So far they're only multiplying. And while most fans barely noticed the 2011 New Orleans Bowl between Louisiana-Lafayette and San Diego State when that year's schedule came out, nearly two million U.S. households were watching when Ragin Cajuns kicker Brett Baer drilled a game-winning 50-yard field goal as the clock expired. The smaller bowls will be fine for as long as ESPN (and perhaps Fox Sports 1 at some point) has programming hours to fill.

The Rose, Sugar, Orange and Fiesta, with 70,000-90,000 seats to fill and armies of devoted volunteers, stand to suffer the most if the playoffs render their non-semifinal games consolation prizes to the participants and their fans. It will therefore be incumbent on the selection committee to create the most compelling possible matchups. "The whole world will be focused on 1 through 4," said UCLA AD Dan Guerrero. "The implications of 5 and down the line are crucial."

That's because for the first time in history a team's résumé will have direct implications for the bowl pairings. Presumably we can all agree that marquee bowl matchups determined by objective criteria are a win-win for everyone in the sport – except, of course, for the fallen bowl scout's expense account.

How Will the Selection Committee Work?

If there's one aspect of the BCS fans may miss the least from the old system, it's the BCS standings. Initially conceived in the SEC's office by commissioner Roy Kramer and his staff, then revised approximately 682 times during the system's first few years, the formula ultimately consisted of three inherently flawed components.

You had the coaches poll, conducted by members of the one profession that may well see the least amount of college football games on Saturdays (because they're coaching in them) and whose self-serving motives include the fact many earn bonuses based on their teams' place in those rankings. "All coaches have an agenda," the *Denver Post*'s John Henderson wrote in 2009. "Their poll is the perfect place to display it."

You had the Harris Poll, a hodgepodge of former players, coaches, administrators and media members that only came into existence because the AP objected to the use of its more established poll. As Big Ten commissioner Jim Delany said in 2012: "Everybody recognizes the present poll system is not a good proxy."

And you had a set of six computer rankings, five of them shrouded in secrecy as to their methodology and all of them neutered due to BCS officials' insistence on removing margin of victory from their data. Jeff Sagarin's respected power ratings become a whole lot less powerful when 3-2 means the same thing as 42-3. "It's clearly an effort to use math as a cover for whatever you want to do," renowned sports statistician Bill James said in *Death to the BCS*. "It's just nonsense math."

In light of the BCS overseers' own acknowledgment over the standings' flaws, the commissioners opted for a radical change when designing the College Football Playoff. They created the sport's first-ever selection committee, a 13-member panel charged with picking not only the four teams for the playoff semifinals, but also the participants in the other New Year's Six bowls. Though a new concept in FBS football, the model should be plenty familiar to college sports fans and media. A selection committee of commissioners and athletic directors creates the 68-team NCAA tournament bracket each March, the FCS playoff field each December and a multitude of other NCAA championships.

The public, of course, is welcoming the new committee with open arms.

"Am I the only one who is nervous about this 'committee' making all these decisions?" an Alabama fan wrote on a BamaOnline.com message board, to which someone responded: "No, you are in good company."

"A human selection committee for the coming college football playoff is a really bad and stupid idea," wrote CBSSports.com's Dennis Dodd. "[Thirteen people] in a room deciding major college football's first-ever tournament like they were secret government scientists poking at an alien corpse?"

"I'm more nervous about a 13-member committee coming out and blowing their selections than I am the BCS," wrote FoxSports. com columnist Clay Travis.

In short, the idea of entrusting a select few professionals to decide which team finishes fourth and which one gets left out is so unnerving to some it makes them pine for the days of uninformed voters and mysterious, mathematically unsound computer formulas.

Oh, college football. Will you ever be happy?

Picking the Pickers

The move to a selection committee originated as a compromise of sorts during the 2012 debate among conferences as to whether the playoff field should consist of the top four teams in the polls or the top four conference champions. The specific language used both at the time of the announcement and as they begin their official duties is that the committee's mission is to "select and seed the *best four teams* for the playoff, and assign other teams to selected other bowl games." Not the best four champions. Not the four most-deserving teams. *The best four teams.* How they ultimately define "best" is the $608 million mystery that will undoubtedly cause mass hand wringing and endless conspiracy theories in the months and years to come, but the commissioners mandated which criteria they should emphasize. "The selection committee has the clear signal that winning conference championships and strength of schedule matter, and those are two of the determining factors if two teams are hard to separate," said the Pac-12's Larry Scott. That alone provides more clarity than the traditional polls, whose primary instructions to voters were as follows: Turn them in on time.

I myself have pretty strong opinions on this topic. For one thing, I used to vote in the AP poll and will freely admit that, even though I took my responsibilities seriously, my rankings were far from scientific. Like most participants, I often cover a game on Saturdays and therefore see only bits and pieces or highlights of other games played during the same time slot. Yet I had only until noon the next day to determine whether Team X was better than Team Y, whether I'd seen them play or not. So like most participants, I often took the teams from last week's ballot and moved them up or down.

On the other hand, I've been part of mock exercises the NCAA holds for media members to see firsthand how the basketball selection process unfolds, and while hardly perfect, it truly is impressive both in its organization and depth of analysis. In 2012, Greg Shaheen, a former NCAA executive who ran the committee, helped colleague Pete Thamel and me conduct our own mock exercise for football using much the same procedure with a panel of ADs from each conference. Believe me, a group of knowledgeable professionals sitting in a room together and carefully deliberating over their selections is far more sound than the hastily produced polls used by the BCS. "I know the importance of looking at data, looking at the information presented to you, really working hard to see things from as many angles as you can, knowing you don't have an eternity to make decisions," said committee member and former White House cabinet member Condoleezza Rice. "... I also know the value of having colleagues who can question you, and you can question them, and you get better quality decisions if you have that collaborative process."

That being said, I'm less than thrilled with some of the initial policies adopted by the football committee, which I'll discuss later in the chapter. Further, I recognize that enlisting a committee to pick just four playoff teams is cause for far more controversy than their basketball counterparts' selection of 68. "It hits you in the face when you start looking at the last couple of spots and how many teams can make legitimate claims for consideration for the last two spots," said Mississippi State AD Scott Stricklin after participating in our mock selection. "It's going to be a daunting task when the real committee gets together."

And finally, no matter how accomplished and respected the committee members may be, it will be virtually impossible to eradicate the perceived personal biases many fans will assume to influence their decisions. Because of course there are no better arbiters of objectivity than rabid fans of a particular team.

"I may have to change my e-mail address and Twitter account," joked committee member Pat Haden, USC's athletic director.

Before further discussing how the selection committee will operate, let's acquaint ourselves with the people who will be doing the operating. It's not like Bill Hancock went and pulled 13 randoms from a 7-Eleven down the street. "We wanted people of the highest integrity for this committee, and we got them," Hancock said at the time of the group's October 2013 unveiling. "Every one of them has vast football knowledge, excellent judgment, dedication and love for this game."

Hancock, who along with the commissioners spent months whittling down an initial list of about 100 nominees, said the group sought a combination of five groups: 1) former coaches, 2) former players, 3) former administrators, 4) former media members and 5) sitting athletic directors. They got at least one of each, including 10 former players, five current ADs, three College Football Hall of Fame inductees and, in total, roughly 230 years of combined experience in college football. Given the considerable time commitment and the inevitable criticism they'll face, it's actually remarkable so many big names signed on.

"I truly felt an obligation," said Wisconsin AD and former Badgers coach Barry Alvarez. "I was able to get a degree because of college football. I was able to make a vocation because of college football. The least I can do in terms of giving back is be part of this committee."

Mind you, they'll be working pro bono.

Hancock said the standard term will last three years, but "some [members] of this first group will have shorter terms and others will have longer terms, which is necessary until we get into the rotation." For better or worse, the initial 13 panelists will be among the most important figures in college football for the near future.

Ladies and Gentlemen, Meet Your Selection Committee

Jeff Long (chairman), Arkansas athletic director: A former college quarterback and, for two seasons in the '80s, an assistant coach at Duke and Michigan (the latter as a graduate assistant), Long rose through the ranks of athletic administration at five different schools before taking his first AD job at Pittsburgh in 2003. In 2008 he moved to Arkansas. In 2012, he garnered considerable attention for firing successful coach Bobby Petrino following a scandal in which Petrino lied to his boss about the details of a motorcycle accident in which his fellow passenger was a mistress he'd hired to work for his program. So the man has a little bit of experience with unpopular decisions. Alma maters: Ohio Wesleyan (bachelor's) and Miami of Ohio (master's). Former college employers: NC State, Duke, Michigan, Rice, Virginia Tech, Eastern Kentucky, Oklahoma and Pittsburgh.

Barry Alvarez, Wisconsin athletic director: A 2010 College Football Hall of Fame inductee, Alvarez coached the Badgers for 16 seasons (1990-2005), leading a long-moribund program to three Rose Bowl victories. He's served as the school's athletic director since 2005, memorably returning to the sideline for the 2013 Rose Bowl against Stanford after his successor, Bret Bielema, bolted for Arkansas. Hey, does anyone know the name of the AD who poached Bielema from Wisconsin? Oh right. He's the chairman of this committee. In another small-world twist, Alvarez played linebacker at Nebraska in the late '60s, where fellow committee member Tom Osborne was then an offensive assistant coach. Alma mater: Nebraska (bachelor's and master's). Former college employers: Iowa, Notre Dame.

Lt. Gen. Michael Gould, former Air Force Academy superintendent: A retired three-star Air Force general and decorated officer, Gould spent his entire career in the armed forces, stationed at bases around the world. A former letterman for the Falcons and assistant coach from 1976-77, Gould eventually rose to oversee the entire academy, serving from 2009-13. In 2010 he was chairman of the Mountain West Board of Directors. Clearly, Gould has made far more consequential decisions in his life than picking the nation's best football teams. Alma maters: Air Force (bachelor's), Webster University (master's). Former college employers: Air Force.

Pat Haden, USC athletic director: A star quarterback for the Trojans in the mid-'70s, earning two national championships, Haden went on to become a Rhodes Scholar while at the same time playing quarterback for the Los Angeles Rams. Take that, Tom Brady. Haden was a longtime TV football commentator, including a stint on NBC's Notre Dame telecasts from 1998-2009. In 2010, he returned to his alma mater to clean up a department ravaged by the Reggie Bush NCAA scandal. He spent much of his first three years publicly defending widely reviled coach Lane Kiffin before abruptly firing him at an airport in the middle of the night following a September 2013 loss. He is therefore a national hero in many parts of the country. Alma maters: USC (bachelor's), Oxford University, Loyola Law School.

Tom Jernstedt, former NCAA executive vice president: Jernstedt spent 38 years at the NCAA (1972-2010) before incoming president Mark Emmert eliminated his position in one of those corporate "restructurings"; he's now a consultant who's worked with the Big 12 and Mountain West. Jernstedt oversaw the NCAA basketball tournament for decades, which included serving as staff liaison to the selection committee. So the man who once chose the members of that committee is now one of the chosen. An inductee to the Basketball Hall of Fame, Jernstedt has his roots in football, having played quarterback at Oregon from 1963-67. Alma mater: Oregon (bachelor's and master's). Previous college employers: Oregon.

Oliver Luck, West Virginia AD: After serving as general manager, president or CEO of sports franchises from the Frankfurt Galaxy (World League of American Football) to the Houston Dynamo (MLS), the former West Virginia and Houston Oilers quarterback returned to his alma mater in 2010. There the former Rhodes Scholar finalist has the pleasure of supervising two of college sports' most well-known outcasts, football coach Dana Holgorsen and basketball coach Bob Huggins. Luck has a son with whom you may be familiar. His name is Andrew. He played a little bit for Stanford. Alma maters: West Virginia (bachelor's), Texas (law degree).

Archie Manning, former NFL quarterback: Manning originally starred at Ole Miss, which not only retired his No. 18 jersey but also set the speed limit on campus at 18 mph in his honor. He spent 14 seasons in the NFL, primarily with the New Orleans Saints, and reached two Pro Bowls before retiring after the 1984 season. Like that of fellow committee member Luck, his NFL lineage continued in the form of two semi-recognizable quarterbacks, Peyton and Eli. Archie remains a noticeable figure in college football, be it as a CBS studio analyst or running an annual family passing academy that employs notable college quarterbacks as counselors (and, in a rare instance, dismisses one for oversleeping). Alma mater: Ole Miss (bachelor's).

Tom Osborne, former Nebraska coach: Osborne certainly could have benefitted from a playoff during his 25 seasons (1973-97) at the helm in Lincoln, as the Huskers won 12 Big 8 championships and three national titles (1994, '96 and '97), posted 18 Top 10 finishes and compiled a staggering 255-49-3 record. Not surprisingly, he's a College Football Hall of Famer. After coaching, Dr. Tom served three terms in the U.S. House of Representatives and ran for governor in 2006. A year later he returned to the university as athletic director, steering the school's move from the Big 12 to Big Ten. Oh, and he hates the University of Texas. (Kidding.) Alma maters: Hastings

College (bachelor's), Nebraska (master's and doctorate). Previous college employers: Nebraska.

Dan Radakovich, Clemson AD: A tight end, punter and student coach for Indiana University of Pennsylvania, Radakovich has spent more than 30 years in college athletics administration. Prior to taking the Clemson AD job in 2012, he held the same position at Georgia Tech for six years. Radakovich also serves on the NCAA advisory committee, a panel of 10 ADs whom Emmert commissioned in 2013 to weigh in on policy matters. This committee's work will seem like a Carnival cruise compared with trying to fix the NCAA. Alma maters: Indiana University of Pennsylvania (bachelor's), University of Miami (master's). Previous college employers: Miami, Long Beach State, South Carolina, American, LSU, Georgia Tech.

Condoleezza Rice, Stanford professor: Rice, who grew up in Birmingham, Ala., the daughter of a football coach and a diehard Crimson Tide fan, was once the provost of Stanford, where she hired former coach and now committee member Tyrone Willingham. Of course, most of the public remembers her as National Security Advisor and Secretary of State under President George W. Bush. And when her controversial appointment to the committee became news in October 2013, a certain Neanderthal segment of football followers identified her first and foremost as … a girl! "All [Rice] knows about football is what somebody told her," former Auburn coach Pat Dye proclaimed on a radio show. Meanwhile, Stanford coach David Shaw said in a *Stanford Daily* article that he and Rice have drawn up plays together to "create mismatches for Stanford's tight ends." So whatever somebody told her, it stuck. Alma maters: University of Denver (bachelor's, doctorate), Notre Dame (master's).

Mike Tranghese, former Big East commissioner: Tranghese worked at the Big East from its inception in 1979 until his retirement 30 years later, serving as the league's second commissioner from 1990 to 2009. Early in his tenure he persuaded the members to invite schools like Miami and Virginia Tech and launch a football league. When the ACC came and stole the 'Canes and Hokies in the mid-2000s, he held the league together with the additions of Cincinnati, Louisville and USF. Correctly sensing it was still a ticking time bomb, he left shortly before the conference destructed for good. Tranghese served on the men's basketball committee from 1996-2001 and as BCS co-ordinator in 2003-04. Oh, and he hates the ACC. (Not really kidding.) Alma mater: St. Michael's College (bachelor's and master's). Former college employers: American International College, Providence.

Steve Wieberg, former *USA Today* writer: An award-winning sportswriter, Wieberg worked at *USA Today* from its launch in 1982 until 2012. He primarily covered college football and basketball, often authoring enterprise pieces on NCAA and other business-side issues. He'll now be serving on a committee with several of the very newsmakers he covered. "I feel a little bit like Ringo and there are four Johns, four Pauls and four Georges in the band," he said at the time of his announcement. I know Steve from our time covering many of the same events; he'll have no problem matching wits and football knowledge with the assorted celebrities in the room. Alma mater: Missouri.

Tyrone Willingham, former coach: Willingham became one of the hottest coaches in the profession while at Stanford in the '90s, twice earning Pac-10 coach of the year honors and leading the Cardinal to their first Rose Bowl in 28 years. In 2002, Notre Dame made him the first African-American coach in that program's history. In his first season he led the Irish to a surprising 10-3 campaign, at which point his career took a sharp turn in the wrong direction. After Notre Dame fired him two mediocre seasons later, he headed to Washington, where he produced five straight losing records, bottoming out at 0-12 in his last season. Alma mater: Michigan State. Former college employers: Michigan State, Central Michigan, NC State, Rice, Stanford, Notre Dame, Washington.

Just Because You're Paranoid ...

The basketball committee is largely anonymous, except for the chairman who goes on CBS after the bracket gets announced. In football, on the other hand, one gets the sense the public will soon know these 13 names much like they do the roster of SEC head coaches or their favorite team's recruiting commitments. Partly that's because of the gravitas of names like Rice and Osborne. But mostly it's because their decisions carry such considerable stakes. If the basketball committee skipped all the way ahead to selecting the Final Four, you'd know their names, too. "I know a couple of ADs said to me there's no way in the world they'd consider this," said Alvarez. "But you better have a thick skin in this business."

I listed all of the members' various college affiliations to show just how many *perceived* conflicts of interest could surface depending on which teams emerge as contenders in a given year. Of course, CFP organizers and the committee members themselves will have you know there's no need to worry. "I think those who have worked at other places have the integrity to step away from those relationships and do what's in the best interests of college football," said Long.

In an April 2014 news conference, Hancock and Long announced with great fanfare a carefully crafted recusal policy spelling out the conditions under which a committee member must abstain from a discussion or vote regarding a specific team. There aren't a whole lot of them. If a school pays you – either as a current employee or as deferred compensation from a previous job – you're out. And that's it. There's nothing stopping Haden from voting on USC rivals Notre Dame and UCLA or Willingham from voting on all the schools that canned him. There's nothing stopping Luck from voting on the school that helped his son develop into a multimillionaire quarterback.

But the committee members aren't nearly as concerned as fans of those teams might be.

"I've got a lot of respect for Stanford … and I love David Shaw – but I think I can be very fair to Stanford," said Luck. "Other than the school I work for that gives me a paycheck every two weeks, I think I can be fair with everyone else." As for the ADs on the committee discussing and voting on schools in their own conferences, Luck said: "I think it makes a lot of sense to ask Barry Alvarez, hey, you guys played Michigan last week, tell us what you think. Tell us what your coaches said. … At the end of the day, if there are conspiracy theories, great, but I feel this group will get it right."

"I can tell you firsthand, from my time on the basketball committee, if anyone dared to cross the line, they were stopped," said Tranghese. "People just don't allow it to happen. To me the highest priority is your integrity."

One reason it might be particularly easy for this committee to snuff out someone who dares attempt to politick is they'll know each other pretty darn well by season's end. Originally, organizers envisioned the committee's meeting several times throughout the year but conducting only a few selection exercises prior to the real thing in early December. "There will not be weekly announcements, like we have our BCS standings show," Hancock said in October 2013. Six months later, he and the committee reversed course and announced they will in fact release their own weekly Top 25 rankings, beginning the last week of October, and reveal them during a primetime ESPN show. Just like the BCS standings. In 2014, the first rankings will come out Oct. 28.

It's a brand new day – that day being Tuesday.

The entire committee will meet in person every Monday and Tuesday for six straight weeks, at the Gaylord Texan hotel in Dallas, where they'll presumably run up one heck of a room service bill. Then they'll convene for the one that counts on the final weekend of the season, announcing their rankings, the playoff bracket and the other New Year's Six bowl pairings on Sunday (Dec. 7 in 2014). "Once we made a ranking, we felt then we needed to make them weekly," said Long. "That's what the fans have become accustomed to, and we felt it would leave a void in college football without a ranking for several weeks."

While understandable, it's an unfortunate decision. Obviously it was never realistic that the committee would go underground the entire season, then emerge on the final Sunday like Moses with the stone tablets. That would be too jarring. But in conducting their own weekly poll, the committee is defeating much of the original purpose behind its creation – which was, most importantly, to differentiate their process from that of the traditional polls.

Feats of (Schedule) Strength

One of the unavoidable consequences of Top 25 polls is confirmation bias – if as an AP voter you decide in your preseason poll that USC is No. 1, Oklahoma No. 4, it often takes considerable evidence to the contrary to change your perception. Case in point: It became apparent early in the 2013 season that two-time defending BCS champion Alabama's defense was not up to its normal stingy standard, while Florida State began crushing every team it played. But voters did not dare displace the top-ranked Tide in favor of the undefeated 'Noles until Alabama finally lost its last regular-season game. "All of the polls in the history of college football tended to reflect what was done in the past, not that particular year," said Big Ten commissioner Jim Delany. "I really like [the committee] because it's based on what people do, not who people are or where people were."

Although it's true the committee's work will theoretically be scrubbed of preseason perceptions, they'll still have their own starting point beginning in late October from which teams move up and down the rest of the way. Just like a poll. If they're doing the job as has been described, the committee's rankings may differ significantly from those of the prevailing AP and coaches polls (which aren't going anywhere), which is sure to create no shortage of confusion. "When you get to the end, people might have a distinct idea of what's going to happen, but based on the results of the last games you might be surprised by what it ends up," said Haden. "What happens in the [conference] championship games could really significantly change a voter's view of who should be fourth." Which is perhaps another reason why the committee felt the need to issue more regular updates. They anticipate an acclimation process.

"This will be different than anything people have ever experienced before," said Hancock. "The season evolves. It's fluid. Teams get better and get worse. Teams get injuries that change their dynamic. Some team played a team that was healthy in September, then another team's going to play that same team in November, but they're playing a different team. And the committee will be able to take all that into consideration and no computer could."

The fact the committee is taking any of that into consideration is a marked change from the traditional polls. So, too, is their stated emphasis on strength of schedule. While AP, Harris and coaches voters gave some consideration to a team's level of competition, the single biggest determining factor in a school's ranking is usually its number of losses. With few exceptions, undefeated trumps one loss, one loss trumps two losses, two losses trump three. If a Top 10 team loses on a last-second field goal to another Top 10 team, voter patterns hold that the losing team is now suddenly four to six spots worse than it was the week before – even if the teams that moved ahead of it spent the week beating up on FCS or mid-major foes.

By contrast, in the playoff era, it's well within the realm of possibility that an 11-2 team that faced a particularly treacherous schedule may beat out a 12-1 team that feasted on subpar foes. At which point the nation's collective freakout will register a 3.1 on the Richter scale. But again – this is a good thing. It could motivate the nation's premier programs to beef up their non-conference schedules, in turn creating more appealing games for fans. The coming playoff has already caused several programs to schedule high-profile future series, particularly in the Big Ten, which will go from eight to nine conference games in 2016 (joining the Big 12 and Pac-12) and is discouraging members from scheduling FCS opponents. "You can't do anything about your conference schedule," said Alvarez. "It's your intent – where you go to find your [non-conference] games. It's pretty easy for me to take a look at a schedule and see what the intent of the schedule is."

Still, much furor ensued when the SEC and ACC both announced in the spring of 2014 that they would stay at eight games (though mandating that their teams schedule at least one non-conference game against another Power 5 school), fueling paranoia in an already inherently distrustful profession. "If we're going to go into a playoff and feed into one playoff system, we all need to play by the same rules," Stanford's Shaw said following the SEC's announcement. "… We're playing nine out of 12 teams in our conference. Why can't you do the same thing?"

But Shaw's concerns may prove unwarranted. It's teams like his that may benefit most from the new system. In 2013, the Cardinal went 11-2 in the regular season, won the Pac-12 championship and finished fifth in the BCS standings while playing the nation's fourth-toughest schedule, according to Sagarin's ratings. They won six games against Sagarin's Top 30 teams and probably would have garnered serious playoff consideration. Meanwhile, a one-loss team above them, Alabama, did not win its conference and beat just two Top 30 foes.

"The proof will be in the pudding over time," said the Pac-12's Scott, "but I believe more often than not, we're going to get the benefit of the doubt if our team is closely situated to others. And the strength of schedule we have will be the determining factor where our team gets the nod." When the day inevitably comes that a Pac-12 team beats out an SEC team for the last playoff spot, you can be sure of two things: 1) Callers to *The Paul Finebaum Show* the next day will utter things never before heard on radio and 2) the SEC will go to nine conference games, stat.

In the meantime, imbalanced schedules among the various conferences – and in some cases, within the same conference – could cause one of the committee's toughest challenges. In the Big 12, it's fairly easy to determine the best team by season's end. The 10 teams all play each other. By contrast, in the 14-team SEC, teams play just two of seven schools from the opposite division. Ditto the ACC and, in 2014 and '15, the Big Ten. "People are not playing the same schedules," said Tranghese. "Someone can say, 'This conference is the second-toughest conference in the country.' That doesn't mean anything to me. It's who you played."

For example, in 2013, Missouri won the SEC East with an 11-1 record; prior to the conference championship game, however, the Tigers did not play the three highest-ranked teams in the West (Auburn, Alabama and LSU) and lost to the highest-ranked team in their own division (South Carolina). Their best wins to that point came against 8-4 Georgia and 8-4 Texas A&M, and they played Murray State, Toledo, Indiana and Arkansas State outside their league. Had they beaten Auburn in the SEC title game, they almost certainly would have played in the BCS National Championship Game. A selection committee may have felt differently. "To the selection committee, whether or not a team plays eight or nine conference games is inconsequential," said Hancock. "What matters is everybody's schedule as a whole, all 12 or 13 games."

It's the Football, Stupid

Mind you, committee members will not be looking solely at scores and schedules. They do plan to watch actual football games. Lots and lots of them, in fact. The CFP staff has outfitted each of them with an iPad for that specific purpose and has enlisted the conferences and DragonFly, a video scouting service used by many college programs, to ensure they'll have access to both TV broadcasts and coaches' film cutups to watch at their convenience. "My Sundays are going to be entirely devoted to this process," said Haden.

Meanwhile, a company called SportsSource Analytics is developing a data platform that will allow members to sort teams by "hundreds" of statistical categories. Committee members got a preview at one of their 2014 offseason meetings. "We asked them to take all this data and go back as far as they could, 13 to 15 years, and take all the hundreds of categories they have – third and 1 in the fourth quarter inside the 20 – and rank those categories in terms of their relationship to national champions and Top 10 teams," said Luck. "Is it like people always think? Turnover ratio? Rushing yards? Rushing yards against? What I'm going to focus on is those categories that historically have proven to be a common thread of championship teams."

And yet, no can for say for certain until they do it the first time how exactly the various members will define "best four teams." Other than heeding the aforementioned criteria (e.g., strength of schedule, head-to-head results), organizers have made it clear the individual committee members will have freedom to decide how exactly he or she evaluates a football team. "There won't be a single metric like the RPI, which is vastly overrated for basketball," said Hancock.

Will the committee members rely instead on more advanced metrics like *Football Outsiders'* F/+ efficiency rankings? Will it be more a case of the always-ambiguous eye test? "Everyone there brings a little bit different insight," said Alvarez. "Having broken down film, I think I know a little bit about football and what constitutes a good team."

The committee has promised transparency, and Long, as chairman, will go on ESPN every Tuesday night and explain the committee's rationale. But there will be no reporter in the room. There will be no individual voter Top 25 ballots to release, because that's not how it works. Instead, the committee will evaluate small clusters of teams against one another and conduct numerous micro-ballots to produce the larger rankings. For a group whose decisions will affect the livelihoods of countless coaches and players and the ensuing happiness or dejection of millions of fans, the College Football Playoff selection committee is destined to become one of sports' most overanalyzed and second-guessed set of decision-makers. Some years the field may settle itself with relative ease, but often, there simply won't be a right answer.

"These will be very difficult decisions," said Hancock, who's gone back and analyzed past seasons (as I will in just a bit). "The decision in some years between 4-5-6 would have been excruciating. Some years the decision between 3-4-5 would be excruciating. However it falls, this year, next year, or the year after will be difficult. We didn't create the playoff to remove contention. We knew contention would continue to be part of it."

But now you can direct that contention at 13 willing individuals rather than a set of 160-plus voters and a set of mysterious computer formulas. It's an improvement. Really. You just might not feel that way Dec. 7 if your team gets left out.

2009-13: A Playoff Case Study

Over the past decade, "Bracketology" has become its own cottage industry within the college basketball media sphere. Experts like ESPN's Joe Lunardi, CBS Sports' Jerry Palm and others spend the weeks leading up to Selection Sunday constantly publishing, revising and republishing their latest projected brackets. TV talking heads spend pregame and halftime segments emphatically declaring that Gonzaga is now in and St. Joe's is now out of a bracket that the actual basketball committee hasn't even begun devising. Yet come Sunday night, Lunardi and Palm rarely miss on more than one or two of the 36 at-large selections and get within one seed line of correctly placing at least two-thirds of the bracket.

The truth is, anyone can be a successful Bracketologist by taking the time to understand the committee's published policies, but mostly, by studying precedent. We've had 30 years of seeded basketball brackets with at least 64 teams. Archival RPI data is available back to 1991. While the actual committee members change every few years, their tendencies remain relatively consistent. They place great emphasis on non-conference strength of schedule. And there are certain RPI thresholds above which a team rarely gets left out and below which a team rarely makes it. By Selection Sunday, no more than three or four spots are even up for debate.

By contrast, when it comes to the first-ever four-team football bracket in December 2014, we will have zero precedent by which to predict what the selection committee will decide. The best we can do is look at past seasons and conduct hypothetical exercises based on the CFP's published criteria, which state: "[The committee] will emphasize obvious factors like win-loss records, strength of schedule, conference championships won, head-to-head results and results against common opponents." Presumably the committee members will form a general hierarchy based on the teams' records and watching them play, but those aforementioned factors – most notably strength of schedule and conference championships – will be used as an unofficial tiebreaker between closely bunched teams.

With all of that in mind, let's revisit the last five seasons pre-play-off, 2009-13, and conduct some hypothetical selection exercises.

In embarking on the research, I was most curious to find out A) how frequently the Playoff four would differ from the BCS's top four and B) just how many teams in a given year had a legitimate argument for the fourth spot. I used the final BCS standings from each season to narrow the pool to about 10 candidates, but I also randomly re-ordered all but the top two to avoid as much as possible prejudging the anticipated order. The teams' Top 25 and Top 50 records are based on opponents' BCS rankings. Strength of schedule ratings come from Palm's site CollegeBCS.com, which uses a formula very similar to basketball's RPI (two-thirds opponents' records, one-third opponents' opponents' records.) Ideally, I'd use a more advanced metric, but the BCS is the only one I could find in which past seasons' data don't include the bowl games.

In fact, the trickiest part of this entire exercise is trying to avoid judging the teams on their subsequent bowl performances, many of which you may remember well. But they will not yet have taken place at the time our imaginary committee makes its selections, so you may have to suspend disbelief on a few occasions in the pages that follow.

2009

Team	Record	SOS	vs. Top 25	vs. Top 50	Championship
Alabama	13-0	4	3-0	9-0	SEC
Texas	13-0	16	2-0	5-0	Big 12
Boise State	13-0	90	1-0	2-0	WAC
Cincinnati	12-0	54	3-0	4-0	Big East
Georgia Tech	11-2	37	1-1	5-2	ACC
Iowa	10-2	18	3-1	3-2	
Florida	12-1	7	1-1	8-1	
TCU	12-0	69	2-0	3-0	MWC
Ohio State	10-2	34	3-1	4-1	Big Ten
Oregon	10-2	2	4-2	5-2	Pac-10

Alabama and Texas, as undefeated major-conference champions, are the seemingly obvious top two seeds. However, Cincinnati has a decent head-to-head argument with the Longhorns. The Bearcats have more top-flight victories, including an impressive 28-18 out-of-conference win at 8-4 Oregon State. They also won 45-44 in the snow at 9-3 Pittsburgh the last week of the season with a conference title on the line for both teams. Texas, by contrast, had just one Top 25 win – a thorough 41-14 demolition at 9-3 Oklahoma State – prior to surviving Nebraska, 13-12, on a last-second field goal in the Big 12 title game. Huskers star defensive tackle Ndamukong Suh exposed Texas's suspect offensive line in that game. However, the 'Horns played a tougher overall schedule and fielded the nation's No. 3 defense, whereas Cincinnati's was a worrisome 48th. Texas gets penciled in for the No. 2 seed.

Compared with the two other remaining undefeated teams, Boise State and TCU, Cincinnati played a tougher schedule and has more quality wins. Boise State has the best individual win of the three, a season-opening 19-8 win over eventual Pac-10 champ Oregon in which it shut down the Ducks' prolific offense. But the rest of the Broncos' schedule – which included seven games against teams that finished with losing records – is so atrocious it's hard to imagine them garnering serious consideration for the top four. This will likely be a recurring problem going forward for non-power conference schools. TCU, on the other hand, posted the nation's No. 1 defense, notched a 14-10 win at ACC division champ Clemson and clobbered 10-2 BYU (38-7) and 9-3 Utah (55-28). Separating Cincinnati and TCU is extremely difficult. The ex-coaches in the room would probably advocate for TCU due to its elite defense. Others may be swayed by the Bearcats' stronger competition.

Meanwhile, Tim Tebow-led Florida played a Top 10 schedule and posted more Top 50 wins than any team but Alabama, which handed the Gators their sole defeat, 32-13, in the SEC title game. Here, the committee faces a difficult decision whether one-loss Florida's overall résumé is so strong as to push it above undefeated teams and/or teams that did win their conference. Though the Gators had lots of good wins, their sole Top 25 victory came at 9-3 LSU, 13-3. Cincinnati had three such wins.

Meanwhile, though Oregon lost twice, it won its conference and played the nation's second-toughest schedule. The Ducks would merit consideration, but their head-to-head loss to another contender, Boise State, could be a deal breaker. Two-loss Big Ten champ Ohio State also has a case; however, one of its losses was to 5-7 Purdue. Iowa actually has a stronger résumé than the Buckeyes but lost head-to-head and thus lost out on their conference's title.

In the end, there are three serious candidates – Cincinnati, TCU and Florida – for the last two spots. The Gators' SOS is far superior to the other two and therefore negates the fact they did not win their conference. The SOS difference between Cincinnati and TCU isn't huge but the Horned Frogs played just five teams that finished with winning records. That's a tough sell, even if a committee member's eyeball test says defensively dominant TCU was the slightly better team.

BCS Top Four:

1. Alabama
2. Texas
3. Cincinnati
4. TCU

Committee Top Four:

1. Alabama
2. Texas
3. Florida
4. Cincinnati

Cue the outrage!

One year in and you can already see how difficult some of these choices will be. I could make a case for any of the last three – Florida, Cincinnati and TCU. I also can't honestly say that Florida's subsequent 51-24 Sugar Bowl rout of the Bearcats isn't subconsciously affecting my decision. But if strength of schedule is truly as much of a factor as the committee says it will be, then the Gators really do separate themselves.

This result also differs from the BCS-era assumption that the loser of a conference title game is automatically out of the national title conversation. This was a particularly unusual situation in that the SEC title game was a matchup of two undefeated teams, which has never happened before or since. Also, no other team in the country finished with exactly one loss, and the other undefeated contenders played particularly weak schedules. Florida is the correct choice, but the Gators might not have been so fortunate in another season with a different set of contenders.

2010

Team	Record	SOS	vs. Top 25	vs. Top 50	Championship
Auburn	13-0	4	6-0	6-0	SEC
Oregon	12-0	72	2-0	5-0	Pac-10
Oklahoma	11-2	3	3-2	6-2	Big 12
Arkansas	10-2	6	4-2	4-2	
Ohio State	11-1	42	0-1	4-1	Big Ten*
Michigan St.	11-1	50	1-0	4-1	Big Ten*
Wisconsin	11-1	69	1-1	4-1	Big Ten*
Stanford	11-1	57	1-1	5-1	

TCU	12-0	68	1-0	4-0	MWC
Boise St.	11-1	47	2-1	3-1	WAC*
* co-champ					

This was another year where the BCS's Top 2 was fairly clear: Auburn vs. Oregon. Interestingly, the Ducks' numbers are not all that different from those of the other remaining undefeated team, TCU. Oregon was an offensive juggernaut that scored at least 42 points in all but two games and throttled 11-1 Stanford, 52-31. The Horned Frogs' signature win was a 47-7 blowout at then-undefeated Utah, which finished 10-2. Their best non-conference win came at home, 45-10 against 7-5 Baylor. Oregon went to Tennessee, albeit against a 6-6 Vols team, and won 48-13. The Ducks remain No. 2 over TCU, but by a closer margin than you might expect.

Another interesting wrinkle to this season is that two of the most impressive résumés belonged to two-loss teams, Oklahoma and Arkansas. The Razorbacks don't have much of a case since they didn't even win their division and allowed 65 points in a loss to Auburn. The Big 12 champion Sooners are more intriguing. They throttled 9-4 Florida State 47-17; ended the season with consecutive wins away from home over 10-win teams Oklahoma State and Nebraska; and their losses were on the road to 10-2 Missouri and 9-3 Texas A&M. The latter, an ugly 33-19 defeat, could prove costly, though.

Amongst the three 11-1 Big Ten co-champs, Michigan State defeated Wisconsin, which in turn defeated Ohio State, which did not play the Spartans. Ohio State doesn't have much of a case, and though Michigan State holds the head-to-head edge over Wisconsin, its 37-6 loss at 7-5 Iowa is hard to overlook. Wisconsin by contrast ended the season scoring 83 and 70 points in two of its last three games and had a powerful rushing offense, as well as a solid defense led by star J.J. Watt. The Badgers get the nod among those three. But do they deserve to stay above Oklahoma? And what about Stanford? The Andrew Luck-led Cardinal won eight games by at least 20 points.

Stanford, Wisconsin and Oklahoma all have an argument for the fourth spot. The Badgers and Cardinal ended the year on seven-game winning streaks, Oklahoma four. While it's likely a two-loss team will trump a one-loss team at some point, the committee would have to justify placing the Sooners above five of them. That seems unlikely.

BCS Top Four:
1. Auburn
2. Oregon
3. TCU
4. Stanford

Committee Top Four:
1. Auburn
2. Oregon
3. TCU
4. Wisconsin

Choosing Wisconsin over Stanford was not that difficult, both because the Cardinal lack a marquee win like the Badgers' 31-18 win over 11-1 Ohio State and because Stanford did not win its conference. The tougher call is between Wisconsin and Oklahoma. If the committee opts to send a message about the importance of strong scheduling – "intent," as Wisconsin's own Barry Alvarez put it – they might ding the Badgers for playing 2-11 UNLV, 1-12 San Jose State and FCS foe Austin Peay. By contrast, OU played Florida State, 8-4

Air Force and faced Cincinnati on the road. Meanwhile, the Sooners' conference championship game gave them an additional Top 25 win, whereas Wisconsin ended the season beating up on mediocre Big Ten teams. Funny, the situation would be reversed today. The Big Ten now has a championship game and the Big 12 does not.

But ultimately, it's about picking the four *best* teams, and you would have been hard-pressed to argue Oklahoma was playing better than Wisconsin. The Badgers were steamrolling people by season's end. They'd beaten one 11-win team and suffered their only loss to another back in early October. The Sooners lacked a win of that caliber, had two slightly worse losses and had questions on defense, allowing 41 points to Oklahoma State in their second-to-last game.

One final thought: As you may recall, Boise State in 2010 opened the season with a neutral-site win over eventual 11-2 ACC champ Virginia Tech and carried a Top 5 national ranking all the way up to a Nov. 26 game at Nevada, in which the Colin Kaepernick-led Wolf Pack rallied to stun the Broncos in overtime. Had Kyle Brotzman made a chip-shot field goal and Boise remained undefeated, it's very likely the Broncos, out of the now-defunct WAC, would have landed the fourth spot. Today, the stars would have to align perfectly for the 2014 equivalent of that Boise State team to make the four-team field.

2011

Team	Record	SOS	vs. Top 25	vs. Top 50	Championship
LSU	13-0	1	6-0	8-0	SEC
Alabama	11-1	11	3-1	6-1	
Clemson	10-3	19	3-1	5-2	ACC

Boise St.	11-1	39	1-1	3-1	
Oregon	11-2	32	1-2	3-2	Pac-12
Oklahoma St.	11-1	4	4-0	8-1	Big 12
Stanford	11-1	41	1-1	4-1	
Wisconsin	11-2	45	3-1	4-1	Big Ten
Arkansas	10-2	40	2-2	5-2	
Kansas St.	10-2	16	2-2	6-2	

This was the season many feel prompted the end of the BCS. I argued it vigorously then, and the numbers here only reinforce it: Oklahoma State was clearly more deserving of the BCS title game spot opposite LSU than was Alabama. Granted, the Crimson Tide fielded one of the most dominant defenses in the sport's history, allowing 8.8 points per game, and churned out a slew of NFL first-rounders (seven in the next two drafts). They would wind up throttling LSU 21-0 in their rematch. But had there been a BCS selection committee in 2011, I firmly believe they would have anointed the Cowboys No. 2 behind the Tigers.

In fact, this season would actually fall on the easier side as four-team selections go. While Boise State and Stanford are the only other teams besides the aforementioned trio with fewer than two losses, Oregon beat the Cardinal, 53-30, on the road and went on to win the Pac-12. The Ducks have an out-of-conference loss, but that loss came to No. 1 LSU, 40-27, in the season opener. They logically rank above Stanford on the board. And the other contenders are all too flawed. ACC champ Clemson, which started 8-0, might have had a shot, but the committee would not look favorably on its late-season blowout losses to NC State (37-13) and South Carolina (34-13). Ditto Kansas State, a 58-17 loser to 9-3 Oklahoma. Boise State once again came within a missed last-second field goal of another undefeated season, but this one, to 10-2 TCU, cost the Broncos a conference title.

Big Ten champ Wisconsin, led by Russell Wilson and Montee Ball, has the best remaining case. One could see the committee noting how the Badgers avenged their heartbreaking regular-season loss to 10-3 Michigan State on a Hail Mary with their subsequent 42-39 conference title game victory over the Spartans. But a 33-29 loss to 6-6 Ohio State is harder to explain away. By contrast, Oregon's second loss was to 10-2 USC.

BCS Top Four:

1. LSU
2. Alabama
3. Oklahoma State
4. Stanford

Committee Top Four:

1. LSU
2. Oklahoma State
3. Alabama
4. Oregon

First of all, poor Stanford. This is the second straight season in which the BCS considered the Cardinal a top four team but my imaginary committee did not. Condoleezza Rice would no doubt be ticked when she returned to the room. However, conference championships are purportedly a point of emphasis. Oregon, not Stanford, won the Pac-12's.

The two at-large teams I've included to date, Florida in 2009 and Alabama in 2011, were one-loss SEC teams with schedules ranked seventh and 11th, respectively. This trend would of course lead to all manner of bellyaching outside the South, but every season is different. While Arkansas coach Bret Bielema predicted in May 2014 that the SEC "will get a minimum of two teams in the four-team playoffs," that's hardly an annual guarantee. Not every SEC schedule is created equal, as you're about to find out.

2012

Team	Record	SOS	vs. Top 25	vs. Top 50	Championship
Notre Dame	12-0	5	3-0	4-0	
Alabama	12-1	30	3-1	4-1	SEC
Oregon	11-1	24	1-1	7-1	
Florida State	11-2	85	1-1	1-1	ACC
Florida	11-1	1	4-1	5-1	
Georgia	11-2	40	1-2	2-2	
LSU	10-2	16	2-2	4-2	
Texas A&M	10-2	11	1-2	3-2	
S. Carolina	10-2	13	2-2	4-2	
Kansas State	11-1	33	2-0	6-1	Big 12*
Stanford	11-2	2	5-1	7-2	Pac-12

* co-champ

This season – one in which 12-0 Ohio State was ineligible for the postseason – would be an absolute mess. I found this out firsthand when we convened our mock panel of ADs the last week of the season.

Undefeated Notre Dame and SEC champion Alabama were a fairly obvious 1-2 and remain so to this day. Yes, the Irish had their skeptics at the time due to their many ugly, low-scoring wins, and yes, those skeptics would eventually be validated when Eddie Lacy ran over Manti Te'o and the Irish, 42-14. But few could argue at the time that Notre Dame didn't earn its top billing. It went undefeated against a schedule consisting of 10 bowl-eligible teams, including 11-2 Stanford and 10-2 Oklahoma. Alabama's schedule had its share of dead weight, but it managed to beat 10-2 LSU on the road and 11-2 Georgia at a neutral site. It also clobbered Top 25 foe Michigan, which finished 8-4, in the season opener.

After that, though, our ADs made decent cases for at least seven other teams. One popular candidate was Texas A&M, which scored arguably the most impressive win of the season, a 29-24 upset at then-No. 1 Alabama. But if you get caught up too much in that one game, you miss the fact that Johnny Manziel and the Aggies lost at home to the two other elite teams on their schedule, Florida and LSU, and in fact beat just one other conference team with a winning record, 8-4 Mississippi State. Much the same can be said for Georgia, which, if not for a last-second deflected pass, might have beaten Alabama in the SEC championship game and reached the BCS title game. But the then third-ranked Dawgs did not pull it off.

They lost 35-7 at South Carolina and beat just two teams all year that finished with winning records.

Amidst that clump of SEC teams, the most impressive résumé belongs to a team Georgia beat. Florida did not win its division but it did play the nation's toughest schedule, beating 10-2 Texas A&M, 10-2 LSU, 10-2 South Carolina and 11-2 Florida State. Despite the smoke-and-mirror nature to of several of its wins – like beating South Carolina 44-11 while gaining just 183 yards of offense – the Gators earn the third spot.

Two other one-loss teams, Oregon and Kansas State, remain on the board. The Ducks were the most dominant team in the country, rolling up one 50-plus point outing after another, until running into Stanford in their second-to-last game. The visiting Cardinal silenced Oregon 17-14 in overtime and went on to win the Pac-12 championship. After a rough 4-2 start, Stanford switched quarterbacks and ended the season with seven straight wins, the last four over Top 20 foes Oregon State (9-3), Oregon (11-1) and, on back-to-back weeks, UCLA (9-4). In fact, Stanford beats out Oregon in three of the stated criteria – head-to-head, strength of schedule and conference championships. It's a coincidental reversal of the 2011 season, when 11-2 Oregon trumped 11-1 Stanford. Like those Ducks, these Cardinal also lost to the No. 1 team, Notre Dame, on the road in overtime. As for Kansas State, the Big 12 champs have a strong overall résumé but suffer from an embarrassing 52-24 loss at 7-5 Baylor in their second-to-last game. The Wildcats got no love from our mock committee. "I just think Texas A&M and Oregon would beat 'em," said Ohio State AD Gene Smith.

BCS Top Four:

1.   Notre Dame

2.   Alabama

3.   Florida

4.   Oregon

Committee Top Four:

1.   Notre Dame

2.   Alabama

3.   Florida

4.   Stanford

This was the second straight season in which one of the semifinal games would be a regular-season rematch (LSU-Oregon in 2011, Notre Dame-Stanford in '12). Meanwhile, the other edition would be an SEC showdown featuring two teams that didn't meet in the regular season. Crazily enough, that scenario is possible. Thanks, realignment.

2013

Team	Record	SOS	vs. Top 25	vs. Top 50	Championship
Florida State	13-0	61	2-0	4-0	ACC
Auburn	12-1	6	4-1	7-1	SEC
UCF	11-1	81	1-1	3-1	American
Stanford	11-2	3	4-1	8-1	Pac-12
Alabama	11-1	50	2-1	5-1	
Michigan St.	12-1	62	1-0	5-1	Big Ten
Baylor	11-1	38	1-1	4-1	Big 12
Ohio State	12-1	56	1-1	4-1	
Missouri	11-2	13	2-2	4-2	

It was the Year of "… But Who Have They Played?" Heading into the final weekend of the regular season there was great debate about whether a one-loss SEC champion should pass undefeated Ohio State, what with the Buckeyes' weak schedule. In truth, No. 1 Florida State's was even worse, but the 'Noles had been so dominant – winning every game by 17 or more points – few could question their legitimacy. Michigan State's subsequent Big Ten title game upset of Ohio State rendered the schedule issue moot and made for a relatively clean FSU-Auburn matchup. Picking four would have been considerably more dicey.

Most after-the-fact projections – including the hypothetical 2014 bowl lineups I used earlier in this book – assumed Alabama as the No. 3 seed. The Tide were undefeated right up until Auburn's Chris Davis made his miraculous 109-yard return of a missed field goal to win the Iron Bowl. But the Tide's résumé was thinner than in seasons past, including their controversial 2011 campaign. By failing to reach the SEC championship game, Nick Saban's team did not get to play any of the top five teams in the East division (Missouri, South Carolina, Georgia, Vanderbilt and Florida). Its best wins came against 9-3 LSU, 8-4 Virginia Tech and 8-4 Texas A&M, and its normally dominant defense showed weak spots, particularly in the secondary. The question is whether anyone else was more impressive.

Big Ten champion Michigan State fielded the nation's top defense and scored a marquee victory in toppling the Buckeyes. Prior to that, though, the Spartans' best wins came against a trio of uninspiring 8-4 teams. Big 12 champ Baylor racked up a whole lot of points and yards against overmatched foes but beat just one Top 25 team, 10-2 Oklahoma (41-12), and got crushed at 10-2 Oklahoma State (49-17).

Meanwhile, Pac-12 champion Stanford makes the strongest case since Oklahoma in 2010 for inclusion of a two-loss team. In fact, the Cardinal may be the ultimate test case as to just how much the committee intends to emphasize strength of schedule. Their conference's nine-game schedule plus a championship game provided a staggering nine games against Top 50 foes, including Top 25 wins over 10-2 Oregon, 10-3 Arizona State (twice) and 9-3 UCLA. However, the Cardinal didn't just lose twice; one of those defeats came to a 5-7 Utah team. At the very least they're ahead of Baylor, which had half as many Top 50 wins and a blowout loss. The committee would likely opt for Michigan State over the Cardinal due to the former's win over 12-1 Ohio State, but Alabama vs. Stanford would be far more vexing than in the BCS era.

Ultimately, the Cardinal's loss to Utah proves fatal.

BCS Top Four:

1.   Florida State
2.   Auburn
3.   Alabama
4.   Michigan State

Committee Top Four:

1.   Florida State
2.   Auburn
3.   Michigan State
4.   Alabama

While it's the same four teams, imagine the reaction in the South when Michigan State came in ahead of mighty Alabama – preventing an Iron Bowl rematch, no less. But if the committee can honestly rid themselves of preseason perceptions, they'd likely elevate the Spartans, having won nine straight and having exhibited a much-improved offense, over the Tide, which lost their last game and peaked in early November. Not to mention Michigan State won its conference and Alabama did not.

One closing thought on UCF. The 2013 season provided our first glimpse of the sport's new landscape, with the Knights playing one year in an AQ conference before the American lost its privileged status. UCF was a very good team, as it subsequently showed in a Fiesta Bowl rout of 11-1 Baylor, and boasted road wins over 11-1 Louisville and 7-5 Penn State. However, its overall schedule – which included five teams with three or fewer wins – was too weak to merit serious consideration. It might have been a different story had the Knights pulled out a home game against 10-2 South Carolina, which won 28-25.

So now you see just how different the sport's new world order could be. My hypothetical committee differed from the BCS on at least one team in four of the five seasons, and the seed order didn't match once. You also got a little taste of the coming controversies. The number of teams with legitimate gripes about their exclusion generally hovered around two per season. The BCS was relatively clean by comparison over the same time period. "I think one and two are clearly going to emerge," said Ohio State's Smith. "But three and four – Oh my God."

When Will It Go to Eight?

Asked about the possibility of the College Football Playoff expanding from four to eight teams before the end of its upcoming 12-year contract, executive director Bill Hancock told reporters in May 2014: "We're not even thinking eight [teams] at all. Really, it's four for 12 years and then we'll reevaluate." In fact, if you type "Bill Hancock eight teams" into Google, you'll find headlines to stories with virtually the exact same quote – given on different occasions – from April 24, 2013; May 24, 2013; November 27, 2013; April 17, 2014; April 29, 2014; May 14, 2014; May 27, 2014; and in all likelihood, several more dates since this book went to press. All before we even get to the first four-team tournament.

Why do people keep asking Hancock about eight teams when his answer never changes? Clearly, no one believes him.

Speculation about a possible eight-team playoff stretches back far before discussions over the new event formally began in 2012. Remember from earlier in the book, Michigan State coach

Duffy Daugherty advocated for an eight-team event way back in 1966. Even President Barack Obama threw his support behind eight during his 2008 campaign. So rather than simply give thanks that the sport's power brokers have finally delivered any sort of playoff, many fans and media are already pining for the next expansion.

Presumably that's in large part because eight teams seems more inclusive. After all, there are now five universally recognized power conferences fighting for four spots. Some assume more playoff games automatically equal more excitement. Heck, many people wouldn't even be satisfied with eight. They want 16.

But most of all, people can already foresee the impending fury over deserving teams' missing out on that coveted fourth spot.

"It's going to expand because they'll never keep everybody happy," Notre Dame coach Brian Kelly told ESPN.com. "I don't know that four is where we're going to finish this thing. I think it's a great entry into where we want to go. Moving forward, I think the focus will be on whether it's eight or 16 or whatever the number is."

"We're not ready for it yet," said Stanford's David Shaw, "but I would love to see it at some point go to eight."

Like Hancock, the commissioners who crafted the playoff are adamant it's not changing – and I'm sure they believe it. "For those of us who put the four-game playoff in place, we view that as the end," said the SEC's Mike Slive. Considering how many different parts had to align just to get it to four – self-interested conference commissioners, nervous bowl executives and inherently conservative university presidents, just to name a few – another radical change would not be nearly as simple to achieve as many believe. They also believe there's one potentially harmful consequence from an expanded bracket. "The regular season is special for those 13 weeks," said Big Ten commissioner Jim Delany. "The expansion of the postseason could damage and undermine the regular season."

Many scoff at that talking point. After all, a 12-team playoff field doesn't seem to adversely affect the 32-team NFL's regular season. Why would eight in the near-130-member FBS?

But I happen to agree with Delany. College football's regular season is by far the most riveting among American sports because any one game can radically alter the entire landscape. A seemingly innocuous Friday night game between Oklahoma State and Iowa State in November 2011 turned that season upside down when the Cyclones stunned the Cowboys. The 2012 Alabama-Notre Dame title matchup arose in large part when then-undefeated Oregon and Kansas State both suffered upset defeats on the same mid-November night. And no recent moment better encapsulated the win-or-else stakes of college football than Chris Davis's miraculous touchdown return in the 2013 Iron Bowl that catapulted underdog Auburn, not No. 1 Alabama, toward the BCS title game.

Four teams shouldn't affect that intensity too much. While one loss may be easier to recover from with two extra spots in the field – case in point, Alabama may still have reached a playoff in 2013 – no team is likely to lock up a playoff berth before the final weekend. However, eight teams could change that dynamic completely. There would presumably be guaranteed spots for the major conference champions, whether they're 9-3 or 13-0. An SEC team that enters the conference championship game undefeated would be playing solely for seeding or home-field advantage. In fact, the later the season progressed, the most important games would no longer involve Nos. 1-4 but Nos. 6-12, much like those 9-7 and 8-8 NFL teams vying for the last wild-card spot.

Sorry, but I don't prefer that version of the sport, nor would many others. And yet, it's almost assuredly coming.

Mountain West commissioner Craig Thompson has long been the contrarian voice among the BCS/CFP overseers, and while hardly as influential as Slive or Delany, he's also more publicly accepting of reality. "I'm probably in the minority in that I don't know we're going to stay at four [teams] for the next 12 years," he said. "I know that's what the contracts say and everybody's following the script these days. We'll see."

Indeed. We'll see. So far the CFP folks' work in developing the four-team event has been highly encouraging. It will be interesting to see how long it takes the public to embrace the shift from polls to a selection committee. And while divisiveness over the four teams selected is to be expected, the excitement over those first-ever semifinal games will likely drown out the noise – at least at first. Just like with the BCS, it's only a matter of time before indignation over the annual selection controversies become deafening. As you saw in the 2009-13 hypotheticals, choosing four teams is often far messier than choosing two. The good news is a team like undefeated Auburn in 2004 will never again be left out. The bad news is fans will be no less sympathetic if 11-1 Auburn gets left out in favor of two other nearly identical 11-1 teams.

And yet, it's a safe bet that the College Football Playoff will be extraordinarily popular – far more so than the BCS. TV ratings for the championship game will probably be higher than any the sport has ever seen due to the intense buildup stemming from the two semifinals feeding into it, as opposed to the often fatiguing five-week layoff before the BCS title game. Which brings us to the real reason the event will inevitably expand: money. That $608 million a year ESPN is already set to pay for the next 12 years will pale in comparison to what an event with four additional games will fetch. If there's one thing university presidents generally agree on it's that there's no such thing as enough money.

My guess: The field will expand halfway through the 12-year deal, in time for the 2020 season. It makes sense symmetrically. At that point each of the New Year's Six bowls will have hosted the same number of semifinals (two apiece), so contracts can more easily be renegotiated. Also, there's a good chance power brokers Slive, 74, and Delany, 66, will be retired, and other commissioners will have changed jobs. A new generation will likely be less resistant to change.

Of course, the entire college sports model is currently in flux what with the NCAA facing serious legal challenges on several fronts. Who knows what college football will look like in 2020, much less 2027, when the 12-year-deal expires? The Nebraska Cornhuskers may be a professional franchise. That's fodder for an entirely different book. In the meantime, all you can do is familiarize yourself with the much more imminent College Football Playoff.

I hope I've helped.

A Playoff Pop Quiz

Welcome to the end of the book. I hope you didn't skip too many pages to get here. If so, spoiler alert: *The hero dies on Page 56!*

Now it's time to find out just how closely you paid attention. On the next page, I've created a fictional set of end-of-season committee rankings. I've listed each team's conference affiliation and designated which ones won their league's championship. Your job is to A) correctly identify the 12 teams that earned spots in the New Year's Six bowls and B) match them to their corresponding bowl. For this test we'll be using the inaugural 2014-15 bowl lineup, in which the Rose and Sugar host the semifinals.

It's like being back in college – without the booze and 1 a.m. burrito runs.

RANK	TEAM	CONFERENCE	RANK	TEAM	CONFERENCE
1	Cal	Pac-12 champ	11	Wisconsin	Big Ten
2	Tennessee	SEC champ	12	Oklahoma	Big 12 champ
3	Virginia Tech	ACC champ	13	LSU	SEC
4	Oregon	Pac-12	14	Texas Tech	Big 12
5	Georgia	SEC	15	Louisville	ACC
6	Minnesota	Big Ten champ	16	Fresno State	MWC champ
7	Stanford	Pac-12	17	UCLA	Pac-12
8	North Carolina	ACC	18	Ohio	MAC champ
9	Ole Miss	SEC	19	Duke	ACC
10	Florida State	ACC	20	Northwestern	Big Ten

I figured I'd throw Cal a bone. This may be the only chance their fans ever have to see their school ranked No. 1.

OK … have at it:

Dec. 31   Peach:_____vs._____

Dec. 31   Fiesta: _____vs._____

Dec. 31   Orange:_____vs._____

Jan. 1   Cotton:_____vs._____

Jan. 1   Rose:_____vs._____

Jan. 1   Sugar:_____vs._____

Pencils down! See the next page for the answer key.

• The two semifinals are obviously No. 1 Cal vs. No. 4 Oregon and No. 2 Tennessee vs. No. 3 Virginia Tech. As the top seed Cal would go to the in-state Rose Bowl, sending the Vols to the Sugar.

• No. 8 North Carolina replaces Virginia Tech as the Orange Bowl's ACC participant. Per that bowl's contract, UNC's opponent is No. 5 Georgia, the highest-ranked available team from among the Big Ten, SEC and Notre Dame.

• Displaced contract champions Minnesota (Big Ten) and Oklahoma (Big 12) are guaranteed spots in one of the other three bowls. So is Fresno State, the highest-ranked champion from one of the non-power conferences.

• That leaves three open spots, and the highest-ranked remaining teams are No. 7 Stanford, No. 9 Ole Miss and No. 10 Florida State. There are no right answers as to how the committee assigns the teams among the Fiesta, Cotton and Chick-fil-A, though based largely on geography I'd go with:

Fiesta: Stanford vs. Fresno State

Cotton: Oklahoma vs. Minnesota

Peach: North Carolina vs. Ole Miss

If your six matchups were exactly the same as mine, congratulations, you are qualified to be a selection committee member.

If you got all 12 teams but have different matchups for the non-contract bowls, don't worry, you still did great.

If you overlooked one of the contract champions – most likely lower-rated Oklahoma or Fresno State – or screwed up the contracted Orange Bowl matchup, you may want to go back and reread "What About the Other Bowls?"

And if by chance you didn't put the top four teams in the two semifinal games I question whether you even read a page of this book – but thank you for the purchase nonetheless.

Acknowledgments

First of all, thanks to Serge Grossman, the friend whom I referenced in the Preface who came up with the initial idea for this book. Chris Brown and Bill Connelly provided valuable insight as I entered the unfamiliar world of self-publishing. I can't possibly demonstrate the necessary appreciation to my devoted copy editor, Merle Singer ... who also happens to be my loving mother-in-law. Chris Johnson, a future star in sports media, was a more than eager researcher.

Thanks to Matt Schnider, Paul Fichtenbaum, Ryan Hunt, Chris Stone and Ben Glicksman for their support of the project. Thanks as well to the many friends and colleagues who offered feedback at various stages of this process – Lindsay Schnell, Brett Kurland, Pete Thamel, Andy Staples, Bruce Feldman and Pat Forde. All those BCS meeting commissioner stakeouts were more fun than I should probably admit thanks to the camaraderie and insight from media friends like George Schroeder, Brett McMurphy, Dennis Dodd, Rachel Bachman, Ralph Russo, Joe Schad and Matt Hayes.

Thanks of course to Bill Hancock, Michael Kelly and the staff at the College Football Playoff for their assistance and patience answering my many questions. If there were a bracket for college sports PR directors, the CFP's Gina Lehe would be the committee's No. 1 seed.

Finally, thanks to my wife and my rock, Emily, whose love and support know no bounds. I only wish our beloved cat Fredo – my football Saturday couch companion – made it to see the playoff he always wanted. This one's for you, buddy.

About the Author

Stewart Mandel is a senior columnist for Fox Sports. He covered the national college football beat for SI.com and Sports Illustrated for 15 years, attending all but the first BCS National Championship Game, He's won multiple first-place awards in the Football Writers Association of America's annual contest. Stewart wrote his first book, *Bowls, Polls and Tattered Souls: Tackling the Chaos and Controversy that Reign Over College Football,* in 2007. Used copies are now available for $0.01 on Amazon.com.

Stewart graduated from Northwestern University in 1998 with a degree in journalism. His infatuation with all things bowl-related can be traced to his attending the Wildcats' first Rose Bowl appearance in 47 years while he was an undergraduate. He's since covered 11 Rose Bowls professionally and remains in awe of the sunset over the San Gabriel Mountains that occurs midway through the third quarter.

Stewart lives in Mountain View, California, with his wife, Emily.